RESONANCE

ESSAYS ON THE
CRAFT AND LIFE OF WRITING

RESONANCE

ESSAYS ON THE
CRAFT AND LIFE OF WRITING

ANDREW CHESHAM
&
LAURA FARINA
EDS

anvil
PRESS

ANVIL PRESS | THE WRITER'S STUDIO — SIMON FRASER UNIVERSITY

Library and Archives Canada Cataloguing in Publication

Title: Resonance : essays on the craft and life of writing / Andrew Chesham, Laura Farina, editors.
Other titles: Resonance (Chesham and Farina)
Names: Chesham, Andrew, 1979- editor. | Farina, Laura, 1980- editor.
Identifiers: Canadiana 20210265655 | ISBN 9781772141849 (softcover)
Subjects: LCSH: Authorship.
Classification: LCC PN145 .R46 2021 | DDC 808.02—dc23

Book design by Derek von Essen

An early version of "So You Want to Write About Race" first appeared on Open-Book.ca on November 29, 2017.

Represented in Canada by Publishers Group Canada
Distributed by Raincoast Books

The publisher gratefully acknowledges the financial assistance of the Canada Council for the Arts, the Canada Book Fund, and the Province of British Columbia through the B.C. Arts Council and the Book Publishing Tax Credit.

Anvil Press Publishers Inc.
P.O. Box 3008, Main Post Office
Vancouver, B.C. V6B 3X5 Canada
www.anvilpress.com

PRINTED AND BOUND IN CANADA

To all those who have taken time to mentor emerging writers, directly or indirectly, in conversation and in books. Encouragement can be the difference between an unfinished manuscript and a finished one.

We would like to acknowledge that this book
was created on the unceded Indigenous land
belonging to the Coast Salish peoples.

TABLE OF CONTENTS

INTRODUCTION

As with writing, the primary joy of creating this anthology has been seeing our initial idea evolve into something that neither of the editors could have envisioned. When we first talked about creating a collection on the craft and life of writing, we saw it as a community conversation that would demystify the writing process. Our plan was to ask writers and publishers: "What's one thing you wish other writers knew?" What we didn't anticipate were the sheer number of perspectives this simple question would elicit.

With the support of Anvil Press, we were able to work with forty-three talented writers on sharing their perspective on writing. In working on our own writing, and working with other writers, we've learned that every writer struggles with something, no matter how many publication credits are next to their name. Though each project is different, each poem is different, each story is different, there will always be obstacles.

Characters face obstacles. Writers do too.

Obstacles make for captivating stories. The thrill is seeing them overcome.

That's what this book is about.

We are writers. We are also the administrators of the Writer's Studio, Simon Fraser University (SFU)'s year-long creative writing program that focuses on building a literary community. Through our own writing practices, we know that sometimes it's a struggle to get words on the page; and through our day jobs, we know that one of the easiest ways to find a way through those struggles is to get the perspective of other writers.

We worked with our essayists on developing their ideas and refining their pieces to a length that could be consumed by the reader in one sitting. We also asked each writer if they wanted to share a prompt or an exercise that could help the reader put some of the ideas explored in their essay into practice. With each author, we offered to chat, brainstorm, and read drafts, with the aim of helping to articulate an idea. While our goal was not to foreground our role as editors, some writers acknowledge this process in their essays.

Our goal was to create a collection that roughly mirrored the writing process. The anthology begins as all writers begin: by coming up with ideas. The essays then follow on through the elements of writing and revising, and the collection finishes with views on publishing from respected literary publishers. The essays vary from personal to academic to instructional. Some essays are meant to give the reader something to think about or try. Other essays are more reflective. They're about what it's like to walk through the world as a writer. They're about identity, belonging, being seen.

The opening essays cover the start of the writing process and offer ideas for collecting inspiration and images and setting yourself up to write. In her essay "In Praise of Daydreams and Laundry," Christina Myers even celebrates the times when you're not writing but still writing, like when you're doing housework.

There are craft-focussed essays on memoir, fiction, non-fiction, and poetry. There are discussions on plot, setting, and what counselling can teach us about character development. Caroline Adderson discusses how character creates plot. Aislinn Hunter relays her difficulties with developing plot as a "voice-driven writer." As she says in her essay "On Praxis," "action without intention leads to flat reading. Action with too much intention feels clumsy and telling." Janie Chang and Joanne Betzler share their experiences on selecting points of view for their books.

There are moments for poetry too. Joanne Arnott invites readers to give "A Moment for the Craft: Poetry." Rob Taylor invites readers to avoid the cult of clarity in "The Power of Adjacency." Leanne Dunic encourages writers to take risks with form and content. Madeline Sonik invites writers to cross genres and incorporate poetry into their prose.

Though organizing the anthology in this linear way, from conception to publication, felt natural, it also has its risks: it can create the impression that the writing process is also linear. That all a writer has to do is conceive an idea and execute it. The reality is that at some point most projects fail — a necessary rupture. As Wayde Compton says: "The rupture, as awful as it feels, is usually the assertion of great opportunity." So, while we may no longer be going in that straight line (we may be back at the beginning of the process), we are still creating, our ideas are developing.

This anthology has been an opportunity to share perspectives and reflect on the many ways writers incorporate themselves into their work. JJ Lee gives tips for creating the distance necessary to write about past trauma. Joseph Kakwinokanasum writes about the tools he's collected in his journey from being told there's "no such thing as an Indian writer" as a child to being a published author. Carleigh Baker relays her experiences with coaxing auto-fiction from tender moments. K. Ho shares their feelings of conflict as they grapple with whether they want to write about their identity as a person with intersecting marginalized identitities.

There are essays reflecting on the role of community and the familiar. Betsy Warland talks about how proximity — the feeling of nearness — helps a reader connect with a piece of writing. Proximity to community also helps a writer develop. John Whatley reflects on writing the familiar essay, in the tradition of Montaigne, while walking through his neighbourhood. Jen Sookfong Lee shares her thoughts on representation and ways to approach writing characters from outside our own cultures and communities. And Fiona Tinwei Lam, in "Giving Voice to Your Words," talks about the value of participating in the writing community, attending public readings, and being gracious and thanking all the people who maintain the literary world. She also encourages writers to forgive themselves for "the occasional blunder or gaffe — we all learn through our mistakes."

The final essays are a reflection on the publishing process from the people writers are eager to engage: the publishers. Leigh Nash writes about publishing as a communal process and the winding path it takes. Andrew Steeves writes about books as extraordinary objects that serve a vital role in communities. Brian Lam writes about how essential LGBTQ+ and BIPOC stories are — not just for those whose communities are being written about, but for all of us.

The principle at work in this anthology is resonance. In physics, resonance refers to the way a sound gets louder when it bounces off an object. In music it describes a sound that is deep, full, and reverberating. One definition refers to richness and variety, another to evoking a response. Our ambition when bringing these forty-three writers together is that their words might resonate with one another, and with the practices and experiences of readers. That the forty-three voices gathered here would not offer one definitive way forward into a life of writing, but instead offer many possibilities: things to try, things to incorporate, things to think about.

We hope you enjoy this collection and find its perspectives and experiences to be helpful for your writing practice. We hope that after you read these essays, you'll find you have your own thoughts on how you create what you create. The experience of creating this anthology has been one of many surprises. We hope that for you, too. That what you create might veer away from what you had first planned. That it might become more than you imagined.

— Andrew Chesham & Laura Farina

AWAKE IN THE WORLD

JANET FRETTER

The humble shoebox is an emblem of my childhood. I was never without one. Each served as a repository for a jumble of collected treasures — marbles swiped from the school playground, chains of pressed daisies, a perfect miniature rubber ball from a long-lost set of jacks. Occasionally I'd take stock, rummage through the box, ranking items for significance. Which objects still gleamed? Which had lost their shine?

Today I carry a small notebook in my purse, or sometimes I cram it in the back pocket of my jeans along with the stub of a pencil. In it I record a cache of sensory nuggets, gathered as I move through the world. It is my creativity shoebox.

I began this practice after attending a writing workshop with author Pam Houston in 2015. As part of her pre-writing practice, she pays close attention to the physical world and records *glimmers*, "little charges of resonance," that she later mines for meaning. She avoids analyzing the sensory image in the moment and simply records the thing itself, trusting that it will unlock something in her writing later. I took this pearl away from the workshop: trust the image. It knows more than I do.

Some images agitate for attention until I can get back to my desk, where I transfer them into a full-sized notebook. There, they function as individual prompts or they cozy up to another random bit, sparking connection and building toward meaning. Other word pictures carry so much heat that I move them directly into a live draft on my laptop. Still, others languish in the mini-notebook until it's filled. I'll flip back, scanning for heat with a highlighter, and discover them afresh.

My pocket notebook is site number one for creative play. Ultimately, its patchwork of captured nuggets offers colour and texture to enrich story or ignite fresh invention. An image may transfer to the page as a bit of description, but it wants to take me deeper — to uncover fresh beauty or mystery, to whisper some universal truth about being human. The invitation sparks drafting, and then I'm on my way. My creativity shoebox is the tool, but the practice begins with learning to be present in the world.

Being present in the world is paying attention through our senses. For the deepest experience of presence, we choose to suspend distraction. But even when many things vie for our attention, we can still act as sensory receptors.

I live a busy, over-stimulated life. Information floods my senses. Cue my brain circuitry: it kicks in to suppress irrelevant stimuli, enabling me to focus on what's important. But I can bypass this automatic sieve at will.

Within the daily bustle, I carve out moments of close observation and register the sensory experience of place. In group meetings, I notice the gestures, verbal tics, body posture, or facial expressions of folks in the room. On a city sidewalk, the moan of a bus transports me to a street in the Montréal of my childhood. On the SkyTrain, I capture fragments of a fellow passenger's one-sided phone conversation. A brief character sketch emerges as I picture who, on the other end of the line, might draw these responses.

Some writers hone the skill of close observation by taking sensory field trips. I regularly take myself off to a destination, often for a walk. I have no agenda, other than an expectation that some sensory images will surface in this place. I do the obvious things: silence my phone, lose the earbuds. If my mind is crowded, I take a minute to ground myself physically — notice the heel-to-toe roll of my feet on the path or the sun on my skin. As I walk, I let the place and its residents speak. Then I find a perch, where I might use sensory prompts to go deeper.

What is the furthest sound that I can identify? The closest?

What pulls at me in my peripheral vision? What does it communicate from this seen-but-unseen space?

What scent hovers? Is it strong enough to evoke taste? Does it transport me anywhere?

Who moves through this space? How does their presence affect me? What is my skin telling me?

Place decides the array of glimmers that activate my receptors. What I notice on a walk is different than what I tune into in a bar, a library, or the waiting room of a doctor's office. Humans and their behaviours are on rich display in these settings. A bartender calls to coworkers loudly, oversharing about his weekend. He comes home with me (figuratively!) as a character whose identity is wholly wrapped up in the legend he's crafted for himself at work.

I notice, I record. And I trust that these shiny bits will enrich some aspect of my writing.

I aspire to Pam Houston's practice of simply recording the thing itself, without interpretation or analysis. For the most part, I do this. But sometimes I find the effect of the image is so strong, I must make a couple of notes about it. Or a metaphor will suggest itself, and I don't want to lose it, so I get it down too. That's okay. It works for me. In this way, my little notebook acts as an artist's sketchbook — a place to capture both the thing and its essence before it vanishes.

A word about method: it doesn't matter.

I use a physical notebook. When words feel inadequate, I'll record a visual moment with the camera of my mobile phone. Others use their phone's voice recorder or note-taking app. Then there are the exceptional few who upload sensory gems to the drive of their faultless memory.

For practical reasons, the notebook over voice recorder works better for me. It allows me to be undistracted by my own voice and unobtrusive as an eavesdropper. Ultimately, what matters is finding a method that is always close to hand and supports direct observation and memory.

The practice of presence and attention delivers its payoff when I sit to write. I mine the collection in my creativity shoebox and find ideas to explore. One vein leads to a character sketch. A palette of images develops setting, realism, and mood. Borrowed fragments of conversation find their way into dialogue, igniting tension and deepening character. Bits of body language weave subtext.

I don't always realize why I've recorded a thing. I noted something about a leather chair. The surface of one arm shone brighter than the other, and I'd scribbled an idea about how objects are changed by human contact. It wasn't until I unpacked the image later that I was blindsided by its real message. My father's reclining chair returned to me, burnished where his elbow massaged it over years of shifting the daily crossword closer so he could enter the conquered word. I could see the headrest hollow where he'd settled his head, a cradle for all those big thoughts. I remembered burying my face there when I returned from the funeral home, breathing in the last of him. A simple recorded observation opened a rich freewriting session and reinforced my conviction that the image knows more than I do.

The image will suggest its own application. Some will develop pieces I'm currently writing, or they may revive stories that are doing drawer time. Others carry such intensity that they spark live invention. On a narrow sand causeway linking mainland Shetland to St. Ninian's Isle, I witnessed the tide rush the beach from two directions, either side of where I stood. An emotionally conflicted character suddenly took up residence in my head. The two-directions theme, so vivid in the moment, quickened story to life.

Some of the richest nuggets will be small phrases that carry worlds of meaning. I capture snapshots of my own understanding — what I infer or intuit in a moment — before they vaporize. Author Kim Stafford calls these "miniature infinities, windows to stars." Mining my little notebook just now, I unearthed the phrase *the elusive nature of redemption*. The context is long forgotten, but the stories breathing in this fragment are many.

As I do the occasional inventory of completed notebooks, I keep anything relevant to my development as a writer — scraps of kindling for future work.

The class of things I collected in the shoeboxes of my childhood changed as I grew. Silly Putty and felt pens were replaced by love notes and concert ticket stubs. I'll always be a collector. It's how I process my world.

An old thing becomes new. Today I channel the habit into a prelude to writing. I'm still on the lookout for shiny things. Now they serve as portals to invention.

PROMPT:
Sharpen your skills of close observation as you move through your day. Stop intermittently, even if it's only for a few seconds, to bring your mind and senses into the moment. The orange you tossed into your lunch kit becomes a sensory experience. Feel its pebbly skin. Look at its colour. Is it the brightest thing in this space? Jab it with your thumbnail and start to peel. Notice the spritz of citrus oil and register its scent. Does it conjure a memory? Is smell mixing with taste, even before the first segment is in your mouth? Pop a piece in your mouth. Crush it, feel the juice burst, taste it. Think of a metaphor for the sensation — sunshine, explosion, a riot, a prism. You won't forget these sensory bits quickly, even if you don't have time to jot notes. When you return to the page, you will connect sensation to memory, imagination, and discovery.

BIRDS OUTSIDE
THE BOARDROOM WINDOWS

RAOUL FERNANDES

Paintbrushes in a chipped coffee mug. "Be here now" Sharpied above a urinal.
A small-town skateboarding ghost with a head wound who rolls up and mum-
bles wise stoner thoughts in your ear. My three-year-old son in a Paw Patrol face
mask. A salt lamp in a Shoppers Drug Mart.

These are some recent images that I've written in my notebook but
haven't yet used in poems. Some of them suggest potential poems
(I think I have something going with the salt lamp); some just hang
around (the poor ghost skater) and wait to be summoned. Many seem
happy never to be summoned.

Paying attention, deeply and mindfully, is one of the most important practices for me as a writer. Both for my outer and inner world.
But it's difficult to do it well. The brain, usually so focused on its
daily business — keeping safe crossing the road, what to make for
dinner, turning over a futile argument — wants to dismiss the irrelevant, impractical micro-thoughts that flit around in the shadows.
They seem useless or even dangerous to focus on (is this why so many
poets don't drive?). But these thoughts and observations are essential
for fostering a creative mind. A lot of them may be absurd, but giving
them time by writing them down can signal to your inner algorithms
that these observations have value. Then the mind slips more easily
into a lucid and attentive noticing. Indeed, interesting images may

often only come to me when I'm writing because I've quieted the more rational, business-like parts of my mind. I've cleared out the executives, opened the windows in the empty boardroom, and let the weird flying thoughts know they are safe to come in.

Images in poems ground me, set the tone, and suggest possibilities. They seem to work better than an abstract "idea" for a poem because of the ambiguity they can contain. A resonant image seems to swirl with associations and meanings, suggesting directions where a poem could go. If I have an image of, say, pushing a friend around in a shopping cart in an empty parking lot, the poem could focus on that friend. The poem could also accumulate related images; could it be a list poem that folds in other images from that town? Or if the shopping cart image arises a young rule-breaking feeling in me, could it lead to another memory of hijinks? And what might that lead to? In a draft, a central image can function as a tether, to pull me back into the poem if I stray too far. Alternately, associated images can add further colour and nuance if a poem feels too tightly bound to one idea or meaning.

Before I go further, I'd like to say that while I'm using the word "image" here, I don't exclusively mean something visual; it could be a sound, a clip of memory, a bit of dialogue — anything distinct that seems to light up one's head. Ezra Pound's definition of an image is useful here: "that which presents an intellectual and emotional complex in an instant of time." I'll focus more on the visual here though because I tend to gravitate to that.

If you are drawn to metaphorical thinking some of the images may form in your mind that way. I'll go through a simple example of that process. Let's say you have a piece of worn sea glass. Thinking about how it slowly gets smoothed out over time may lead you to think about how that happens to people: how the days (like sand and water) wear us down, making us more accepting. In making that connection, you have a metaphor: "his heart smoothed over the years like sea glass." It can also move in the opposite direction; you're looking for something to represent someone's edges gradually being worn away, and that image pops up from your memory. An interesting thing here is that the sea glass = heart link also creates or reinforces a concept of outer world = inner world; things around you can represent something inside you. The more you use outer world = inner world connections — or any another kind of imaginative concept — the more natural it becomes for your mind to make those types of connections. The connective tissue itself strengthens, slowly becoming part of your skill set.

I'm making this idea of attending to images and drawing connections seem very conscious, but it's (thankfully) something that we all do with our intuition and subconscious. The meanings tangled within an image can almost feel like textures, sounds, colours. And from these, the creative mind seems to be able to feel out what to do with them. Just as a musician might intuit what chord comes next, or a painter may follow an impulse to paint an orange triangle in a field of blue. Trusting that kind of fluid feeling and intuition seems vastly important to develop, albeit difficult to really explain or instruct — other than to say reading, writing, and daydreaming a lot seem to help. Take chances, don't be afraid to fail, trust the wildness of your mind. The images that make me most curious, that call up the most questions, are often better to zoom in on than the ones that are more obviously poetic or beautiful.

As a poet, I'm often told: "You should write a poem about that!" I almost never take the suggestion. It feels weird to say, but I get uneasy thinking of going about my day actively seeking out things I can extract and plunk into a poem. It feels like a kind of commodification. I just want the moments and images to have time to sink into memory, grow tentacles, and interact with the other sea creatures, before they find their place in a poem. Or never find their place, which is fine too. Fundamentally, I want to value the act of noticing and being curious outside of simply being a writer. It is what makes us feel alive, lucid, and present as human beings. Whether you write about it or not, it's still wonderful that you stopped to looked at something — that it stirred up memories, lit up your daydream machinery, and caused you to miss your bus.

PROMPT:

Some images are suffused with meaning and possibilities. There are natural ones — such as the moon, ocean, trees, and rain — that already hold a lot of depth. But there are also ones that are more particular to you and what you notice in the world. This is an exercise to discover and channel the potential of such images, by brainstorming and diagramming the creative leaps and associations your mind can perform with an image.

First, of course, you'll need an image, something that has been lingering in your mind or has come up in a poem or story you've been writing. If you're starting fresh, I'd suggest a couple things: walk around your house, or wherever you are, and find an object or image that has some meaning to you. Look at it carefully, and then put it away, and come back to your writing desk. If you are somewhere where this isn't possible, you could look around you or at pictures on your phone until you come across something that sparks your curiosity. Again, look attentively at it, then put your phone away. I'm suggesting avoiding having the image right in front of you because it risks making it too "real" — letting it sit in your memory, I believe, allows it to be more malleable for your imagination.

On a large sheet of blank paper, write a simple description of the image. Just something like "a Little Mermaid backpack" or "goshawk on a power line." Now circle the image and draw five lines radiating away from the image. At the end of each of these lines, write a line or two of something the image makes you think of. For variety, try to hit some of these: a sensation, a memory, further specific details of the image, a completely different but related image, something fantastical. Next, choose at least two of these texts that are the most interesting to you, circle them, draw a few lines radiating out from each of these, and continue to add more writing. Make big leaps, take odd tangents, and cross wires between associations. You can invent ways of visualizing the connections, like drawing longer lines for more distant associations, or a squiggly line for a weirder leap. Play with colours, even drawings, if you like.

Continue with this process a couple more times until you either have run out of space on the page or you feel you have accumulated a satisfying amount of material to work with. From this diagram, take the more interesting chunks of text and write or type them all up. When working on shaping this material, you want to zoom in on the most interesting thing that came up, or you might want to fold in many different associations in your piece. This exercise can function as a way to generate material to use in a poem or story, or simply as good warm up stretches for your creative muscles.

Bonus: You could also use this exercise as a metaphor-creator. Say if your initial image was "moon," you could go "moon" —> "cold, white" —> "snowball" = "The moon was a snowball." This is a straightforward example; some of your wilder associations would create more unusual and interesting metaphors.

WRITING OBSESSED: THE COMPULSION TO WRITE AND STAYING TRUE TO A STORY

KATHERINE MCMANUS

Some writers begin writing because of a story they need to tell. For others, a story comes in search of its writer. In either case, for the writer, it is often such a nagging, insistent experience that to write is simply the easier alternative. Many writers have known the obsession of the one story that needs to be told — whether it is from our own lives or from someone we know, or even from something uncovered.

Michael Crummey has talked in interviews about his reluctance to write *The Innocents*. In interviews, he has said that once, when searching the archives of his home province, he read an account of children who were "stumbled across" by a travelling eighteenth-century clergyman. The clergyman discovered the orphaned brother and sister living in a remote cove on the northern peninsula of the island of Newfoundland, but when he approached them to enquire about their circumstance, the clergyman was driven away by the boy at gunpoint. Crummey was both compelled and reluctant to put together what might have happened to these children. He assumed their parents had both died — not an unusual occurrence in remote villages — and to survive, they lived on instinct and whatever skills they had learned from their parents before they died. It is a story of incredible resilience and horrifying hardship. His imagination of their lives took him to both the brightest and grimmest of possible realities. He gave life to what he imagined because the image wouldn't leave him.

For me, my "compelled to write" moment came while taking a course as a graduate student at the University of British Columbia. I left Newfoundland to pursue a final degree, and in the course of doing so, I discovered the name of an extraordinary Newfoundland woman, Florence O'Neill, who taught adults during the mid-twentieth century. She travelled a unique path to become a highly educated teacher and administrator in the Newfoundland government in the middle of the twentieth century; but by the time I arrived in Newfoundland in 1975, she was already forgotten.

At first, I was simply curious about her. Her name appeared in a textbook for a course I was taking at the time. She was, I learned, one of the first people in Canada to earn a doctoral degree in adult education from Columbia University in New York. She then returned to Newfoundland to contribute in notable ways to the education of adults. Unlike Crummey, I had no hesitation in pursuing her story. I was a "come from away" living in Newfoundland, and island culture fascinated me. I thought I had discovered a true female pioneer in education, and learning more about her appealed to me. I didn't know why she was not well known in Newfoundland — usually, notable citizens gathered a reputation.

An early worry for me was simply how to find information where there didn't seem to be any. Where would I find a trail of her life and work? I had never searched archives and didn't know how to start. But curiosity is a great engine for driving one forward. The need to know what had caused her to be buried and forgotten was strong. The great conundrum for me was that she was well enough known outside of Newfoundland in the field of adult education to be cited as a pioneer; but she was absent from the records of adult education in the province where she worked for decades.

At the time I was a student, but not an inexperienced one. I had already worked for universities and government departments and was fully aware of how difficult it was to influence bureaucracies. I knew that she might have been buried under the weight of department files or by the slow movements of others. And, as a feminist, I wondered if her disappearance from the community *zeitgeist* had to do with the fact that she was a woman.

The compelling story, while dragging you forward into it, also presents you with many dilemmas. For Crummey, his work of fiction came from a deep understanding of the difficulties faced by people living in small fishing communities and the horror of surviving there without parents or family. He also understood the strength of those communities and may have wanted to look for many ways for his characters to be saved by others early in their lives. The story could have gone in a couple directions, but he chose to focus on what the clergyman reported. He knew the result would be very hard to write.

For me, curiosity turned into passion quickly. As I learned to navigate archive systems, I found pieces of information that began to form O'Neill's life. The events and milestones that shaped it fell into place. O'Neill had died only a decade earlier, so there were many human tracks I could follow. People who knew her began to contact me and urge me to keep going. Interviews, newspaper articles, and letters between Florence O'Neill and friends and acquaintances provided a rich context for the more mundane office communications I found in the archives. I heard both the good and the bad aspects of her character, and soon I began to feel as though she was a friend and colleague.

From university, city, and provincial archives, I could trace the formation of adult education in the Atlantic provinces. Also, letters flowed from individuals at the Carnegie Corporation to those in the Department of Education in Newfoundland, creating a chronology of funding, programs, and evidence of support for the education of Florence O'Neill. I followed the money as programs, funded by the Carnegie Corporation, created employment and a need for people to develop programming and administer it. Two important documents formed a strong idea of the person who had been Florence O'Neill.

One was her own dissertation, in which she developed an entire adult education program for Newfoundland complete with programs, job descriptions for those who would be employed, as well as a list of goals and objectives. The other was a transcript of an interview with her about her life. The interview was done by her nephew, a university professor, and it was an attempt to record her early life, her elementary school teaching in villages all over Newfoundland, and finally her experiences as an itinerant adult education teacher posted for three months at a time in remote communities to do what she could to help people to learn to read and write.

The more I dug, the more exciting it was to find the history of a woman who had struggled her entire life to do the work she loved and who believed wholeheartedly in following her passion. But I also began to understand the burden of writing that history. When I started, I thought that I had found a story that, yet again, spoke to the difficulty women face when they work within a public bureaucracy. And I did find that — or at least that is how I reconstructed what I found. As I researched, I realized that I was shaping the arc of her life by the way I put the documents together. My reconstruction of her life might not have been true to the real story. In fact, I was frustrated by her lack of commenting on how she would not have been able to continue to work if she had married — even though she married immediately following her retirement. Or that she did not blame her unequal treatment within the government — her lack of autonomy and privilege compared to male colleagues — on the fact that she was a woman. My passion in reconstructing O'Neill's life was to unearth yet another example of "glass ceilings" in the workplace, but O'Neill was not complicit with my thesis. She resisted it by never talking about her career that way.

My "compelled to write" experience needed to be re-examined and adjusted to fit the circumstances of the history I had found. Many other complexities of status and hierarchy were at play in the politics and culture of Newfoundland in the mid-twentieth century than gender. My obsession with O'Neill had become my story and not hers.

When obsessed or compelled by a story, it is easy to become distracted. Identifying distractions in order to focus on why the story was initially compelling is an important part of the work of writing — in any circumstance, but especially when the kernel of the story was something that infected you with a purpose to write. For Crummey, I am sure that as he wrote *The Innocents,* he looked for an alternative narrative for the children. He must have wanted to find ways for them to be saved, but that wouldn't have been a strong likelihood in their circumstances. While writing, he had a kind of "pact" with what he'd found in the archives, and he needed to be true to it. With O'Neill, once I had begun to find the pieces to her life, I felt her need for me to honour how she thought they would fit together.

PROMPT:
What has been an idea, experience, person, activity, or event that you carry with you and can't put down?

To begin to explore it, do some or all of the following:
- Name it.
- Remember it in the context of your first encounter: when did you first come across, or meet, or do this "thing"?
- Explore it in relationship to your life: why is it interesting to you?
- Explore it in relationship to others: does it have importance in the wider world?
- Focus it: what is the story?

Once you have written around the experience and looked at it from as many angles as possible, think about what kind of writing it needs to be. What is the best vehicle for this writing: poetry, graphic novel, memoir, biography, fiction? You might find that you feel a strong urge to depart from your usual inclination in writing. If so, follow your inclination and explore writing about your "thing" in a different genre from the one to which you usually turn.

Or you might want to try freewriting now. If you've never tried this technique, it is a useful one to learn to begin writing on a new topic or story idea. To freewrite, you use your favourite composition tool — computer, pen, pencil, whatever suits you — and you start writing the first things that come to mind. You keep writing for five minutes. Do not judge what you're writing: just write. After five minutes of writing — whatever passes through your mind about your "thing" — you might find that ideas have come together to help you find your way into your topic.

WRITE ABOUT SOMETHING ELSE: PURGING NEGATIVE THOUGHTS

ANDREW CHESHAM

Your writing is bad. No, seriously. Listen. What you're writing is bad. Are you listening? People will laugh... So, stop. Now. Nobody is making you do this. Stop. Just get up and re-watch season three of The Office *for the third time...*

This is an entry from my pre-writing journal. I used this example because it's typical of the negative thoughts I have about my writing. Most days, I'm my biggest obstacle.

Example: I'll have a great idea. I'll click my lamp, open my laptop, and bam — as my fingers hit the keys — negative thoughts arrive. I'll try to ignore them, the negativity, the voices telling me I have no right to write, let alone call myself a writer. But I can't. I just freeze up. Determined, I will try to write a scene or describe a character. Instead, I lightly tap the keyboard (always the letter "k") and stare at my screen. After twenty taps or so, sick of feeling so critical, I finally close my laptop, stand up, and leave the room — barely a paragraph written.

I'd come back the next day. Inspired. Determined. Then the negative thoughts would join. Another partial paragraph written. Laptop closed once again.

A good day was one hundred words. One hundred painful-to-write words. And for the longest time that's how it was. Seven hundred words at the end of a week, and, maybe, three thousand words at the end of a month. That's it.

To be clear, there's nothing wrong with one hundred words a day. One hundred words is always better than no words. Always. Progress is progress. I try to never forget that.

However, I wanted to write a novel, not a short story. At my current rate — seven hundred words a week — a seventy-thousand-word novel would take me just under two years to write. Two years! I'm for consistency and sticking with it, but I didn't want a first draft to take the same amount of time as it would to read Proust's *In Search of Lost Time* (it would have taken me thirty-seven years to write those seven volumes. I heard he did it in five summers, though I've not looked it up to confirm). In short, I had to get my word count up, which meant I had to get out of my way and face my negative thoughts.

Two things happened. Not right away, but in a short enough time that I was able to have a minor epiphany. First, I read Peter Elbow's *Writing with Power: Techniques for Mastering the Writing Process.* Then I read John Steinbeck's *Journal of a Novel: The East of Eden Letters.* From Elbow, I learned that writing has two stages: creating and critiquing, and these stages need to be separated. Elbow suggests freewriting as a way to generate content. I had been aware of freewriting for a long time (it's discussed in many introductory books and courses on writing), but when I read his take, this passage stuck with me:

We have lots in our heads that makes it hard to think straight and write clearly: we are mad at someone, sad about something, depressed about everything. Perhaps even inconveniently happy [...] freewriting is a quick outlet for these feelings so they don't get so much in your way when you are trying to write about something else. Sometimes your mind is marvelously clear after ten minutes of telling someone on paper everything you need to tell him[1].

When I came across *Journal of a Novel: The East of Eden Letters* by John Steinbeck, I had been journaling for years, though I didn't use it as a way to progress my writing. To write the first draft of *East of Eden*, Steinbeck used a leather-bound notebook given to him by his friend and book editor Pascal Covici. He also used it as his diary. In one of the first entries, Steinbeck explained his aim for the notebook: "I intend to keep a double-entry book — manuscript on the right-hand page and work diary on the left. Thus they will be together." In this manner, he started each day by writing a letter (a diary entry) to Covici, discussing how he was feeling, what section he was working on, what his ambitions were, and what obstacles (in the writing or his daily life) he was trying to overcome. Then he would work on the novel. All within the same book.

Another entry looked like this:

July 6 — I feel just worthless today. I have to drive myself. I have used every physical excuse not to work except fake illness. I have dawdled, gone to the toilet innumerable times, had many glasses of water. Really childish. I know that one of the reasons is that I dread the next scene, dread it like hell [...] I do not often permit myself to get away with nonsense [...] But right now I am giving myself trouble like a stubborn kid[2].

Steinbeck's words resonated with me. His process resonated with me. And even though he was writing to Covici, a real person, Steinbeck was basically freewriting. He was, in Elbow's words, "telling someone on paper everything [he needed] to tell him."

By keeping a running conversation about himself and his work, and working five days a week, Steinbeck wrote up to fifteen hundred words a day and completed the first draft in nine months.

That was the secret. Put feelings on the page. Name the demons.

A double-entry book was what I needed to get out of my own way. While I didn't have a leather-bound journal (I write on a computer, not in a journal), I could have two documents open, side by side, and one would be my pre-writing journal and the other would be my project. I also didn't have a Covici, but I could talk to someone I trusted: I could talk to my grandmother, Peggy McCorkle. She passed years ago, and I missed her greatly — she was so kind, accepting. I could use the journal to stay connected with her.

I could also talk to myself, I realized, since it didn't really matter who I talked to, just as long as I kept my worries separate from my projects, and put them outside of myself.

Now my process looks like this: on my screen will be two documents — the piece I'm working on and my pre-writing journal. I'll start in my journal by writing the date and time and then take five to ten minutes to write: what I'm thinking; how I'm feeling, personally; how I'm feeling about the piece; what I'm hoping to write; what obstacles I'm facing, either mentally or in the piece; and brainstorm possible solutions. Early entries could have started like the sample at the start of this essay. Now, an entry may look like this:

August 10 | 10:03 pm — It's been a busy day, and the last thing I want to do right now is write. Ten at night. I just want to get ready for bed... I'm not feeling great, but I need to get something down. It doesn't matter if it's good or not. Just do it. What am I doing? I'm in the middle of the scene where Aaron and Christine are sitting around the table with the kids. Their kitchen is in the middle of being renovated, so they're eating takeout on paper plates. The plates are soggy... they've been sitting so long. Neither is happy. Aaron needs to tell Christine that he'll be leaving for work again, and Christine needs to tell Aaron that the renovations will be more expensive, and will take longer, than expected, due to rotting floorboards... Or is it pipes?... Don't know. There's something major that needs to be done. For now, I'll stick with floorboards.

Once I feel warmed up, I'll dive into the writing. Sometimes I'll even use my journal to play with a scene: change the setting, the point of view, circumstances, dialogue. Then I'll pull out the parts I like and paste them into my project. In twenty minutes of pre-writing and writing, I can get more accomplished than if I had just sat down, started to write, got frustrated, and gone off to watch *The Office*.

If at any point during the session I start thinking negatively, I'll return to my pre-writing journal and write those thoughts. I'll purge them from my mind, lock them in the journal.

I've found that by writing about my obstacles (both personally and in the project), instead of keeping them in my mind, I shorten the time it takes to figure it out. Yes, I will come up with solutions while on a walk or in the shower, but I find talking about it on the page is as consistent, reliable as rubbing Head & Shoulders in my hair.

I still have good days and bad days. We all will. But in my practice of pre-writing, I can more easily power through the resistance I'm feeling. Some days I will write more in my journal than in my project, but that doesn't matter since even on those days, there's a good chance I'll be able to reach my target word count.

Last year I wrote around fifty thousand words in my pre-writing journal. For the first draft of my project, most days I hit my target of eight hundred words. I was writing almost every day, so I was able to reach sixty thousand words in under three months. A first draft in three months. It felt good.

As my practice has progressed, I've learned that in order to have a successful session, I need to come to the page free of negative thoughts. And this means most days I cannot start writing until I talk to either my grandmother or myself. These conversations have been key. They've helped me write, yes, but more importantly, they've helped me get out of my own way and write about something else.

1. Peter Elbow, *Writing with Power: Techniques for Mastering the Writing Process* (Oxford University Press, 1998), pp.15

2. John Steinbeck, *Journal of a Novel: The East of Eden Letters* (Bantam Books, 1970), pp.162

PROMPT:
Pre-writing journals can take any shape/form/process you like. The key is to externalize the things you're thinking. If you're looking for a guided approach, a good way to start a pre-writing practice is to put parameters around it. For example, start with a document (it can be on paper or computer), set a timer for five minutes, and answer these questions (just to yourself): How do I feel about myself? How do I feel about my project? Do I want to write today? If no, what is the

source(s) of resistance (is it something outside or inside the project)? How can I overcome any resistance I'm facing, both personally and in the project?

Another approach is to freewrite for five minutes and tell some-one all you need to tell them. Make the person you're writing to someone you want to talk to but can't in this moment (like Steinbeck did with Covici or I did with my grandmother) and tell them: what you did that morning/day, what you loved, what you hated, what you're going to be working on, and how you feel about all of it.

Try each approach for at least five sessions. At the end of two weeks (doing each approach five times), reflect on which one gave you a better sense of calm before you started writing.

Note: In either approach you can try writing a section (dialogue, setting, description, etc.) of your project, and if you like what you wrote, copy it over to your main document. If you don't like what you wrote, just leave it in the journal, for nobody to see.

IN PRAISE OF DAYDREAMS AND LAUNDRY

CHRISTINA MYERS

I am in the woods, midway through a hike around the edge of a lake. I am in the car, stopped at a red light. I am half-awake in the middle of the night, or chopping onions in the kitchen, or sitting on a beach in the middle of winter. I am replaying a conversation I had last night, remembering a break-up from twenty years ago, or, sometimes, I am thinking of nothing at all, focused instead on some mundane task in front of me.

And I am also, simultaneously, writing.

There's no pen and paper, no laptop, no desk or chair. But there's thoughts and ideas, scenes and memories, images and emotions: the sparkle of sunlight on the lake when the wind rises up; the smell of the onions on my hands; the echo of some past emotion now recalled, remembered, reshaped again. There aren't even words — at least, none beyond those that bubble up in my mind then disappear again — but it's still *writing*.

We often conclude we have only been successful in our pursuit to write when we sit down at our desk and *work*. And work, we tell ourselves, can be evaluated in specific ways: did we finish the next chapter, or stay at the keyboard for a specific amount of time, or achieve a predetermined daily word count? Success or failure is measured by how well we accomplished these goals, how productive we managed to be.

Of course, nothing would ever be published if we didn't spend time (and a lot of it, at that) putting words to a page. It's why so many writers create routines, like getting up before sunrise to write for an hour before anyone else wakes up or joining a writer's group to provide accountability and deadlines. Most of the visible work of writing is practical, hands-on, routine, and even at times repetitive — and all of that is necessary.

But before we can come to our desks, before we can *do,* we need to let ourselves *be*: to think, ponder, remember, feel, absorb, examine, re-examine, observe, question, and explore. And we do all that in the "in-between" moments of our life — while waiting for lights to turn green and doing up the dishes in the sink — without even realizing it.

This process of letting our ideas simmer and brew, come to the forefront of our minds, and then drift again into our subconscious is a critical and vital part of the writing process, even when it is unintentional during our quiet and idle moments.

In fact, that's when it may be the most important of all.

Maya Angelou once described her habit of getting up in the morning, leaving the house, and checking into a hotel for the day to work in solitude away from the many demands and distractions of home. She brought pads of paper, pencils, a thesaurus — all the well-known tools of the writer — along with crossword puzzles, small games, and playing cards. The latter, she said, were there to occupy her "Little Mind" so that her "Big Mind" could ponder the deeper ideas and thoughts she wanted to explore in her writing. Rather than jump into the act of writing, she'd first sit at the table and play solitaire or solve a small puzzle, letting her mind wander. Eventually, she'd set the games aside and get down to "work" by writing longhand, continuing as long as the words came to her. At home in the evening, she would read and edit the day's pages, leaving her ready to repeat the process the next day.

She didn't consider the hours spent with the crossword puzzles to be wasted or the card games to be useless; she shared the details of this routine without shame or apology. It was part of her writing life — as valuable as putting pen to paper for a first draft or revising and editing — because it allowed her to access the big ideas that she wanted to explore.

When we think of pre-writing, we focus on concrete tasks and practical tools: journaling, outlining, researching, freewriting, brainstorming, mind mapping, timed writing sprints. These are all valuable techniques that allow writers to access the seeds of creation — the images, ideas, and concepts that will eventually become a story or poem or essay — and their visual, measurable nature allows us to perceive them as worthy.

We also assign value to reading as a tool of the writer because we know it leads to learning and growth. Reading serves as a method of inquiry to our own writing. We read and then we ask ourselves: what did I enjoy, what caught my attention, what surprised me, what worked or did not work? We are content to see this not as wasted time, but as part of the larger process that serves both our writing and, by happy accident, our pleasure.

But we give little thought, and even less value, to the work that our brains are doing in support of our writing in all the other moments of our lives. We even berate ourselves for not doing as much "real work" as we ought to. We tell ourselves that going to the beach is lovely, taking a long walk helps with stress, daydreaming in a hammock is relaxing — but these are not necessary parts of our lives as writers because they don't improve our writing or allow our creativity to bloom.

Except, in fact, they do exactly that.

Søren Kierkegaard wrote: "I have walked myself into my best thoughts," and Jack Kerouac said he "daydreamed" his way into his writing. They may have thought they were making simple observations, but their experiences are rooted in science.

Research has shown, for example, that creative thinking improves after a walk and that dopamine released during relaxing activities can boost imagination and productivity. Daydreaming can serve as an "incubation box" for creativity, allowing for high-level planning and memory processing. And those are just a few of the discoveries about the "idle" brain.

Kierkegaard and Kerouac knew what many writers (not to mention inventors, artists, scientists, and musicians) have discovered: that the big *a-ha* moments often arrive while in the shower, or weeding the garden, or taking the dog for a late-night walk.

Like the lost keys that are only found after you stop looking for them and the word on the tip of your tongue that only comes to you hours after you needed it, the answers to so many of our writing dilemmas may simply be waiting for us to stop hunting so intently, so they can rise to the surface. When we can't figure out how to begin a story — or later, how to fix a passage, what word to use, how best to describe a scene or resolve a conflict — it's just as likely that the answer will come while you're folding laundry as it will while staring at your laptop screen.

Many of us feel guilty about daydreaming, lost time, being unproductive. We feel we ought to funnel our energy into "doing," with the assumption that creation is concrete, and we dismiss — even at times berate ourselves — for the parts of the process that seem useless or wasteful.

It may be worth asking if we are overlooking the most important step.

There's nothing wasted in red lights and folding laundry, in quiet moments and mundane tasks. They are as integral to your writing life — certainly to *my* writing life — as a note-filled journal, a tidy outline, a good first draft, a dictionary, or a red pen.

Allow yourself to honour this part of your creative life, cultivate it, value it, even celebrate it. When the time comes to log hours in front of the screen and to keep track of your word counts, your ideas will be ready for you, shaped and crystallized in unexpected ways by your idle mind. And when you get stuck, return to the start of the process again: step away, take a walk, do some dishes, and let your brain continue to write your stories so that you can return to the desk, ready to work.

PROMPT:

Before sitting down to write, spend time on a mundane task. Go for a walk, do the dishes by hand, play a game of solitaire, or people watch in a busy location. Let your mind wander through whatever arises; don't try to track your thoughts as they pertain to your writing, but simply let them rise up and ease away. When you return to your writing, take a moment to freewrite any images, thoughts, or ideas that are present (whether they are about your current writing project or anything else). In the coming weeks, notice when you feel guilty or when you berate yourself about "wasted" time, and try to re-evaluate that thought process to shift towards understanding the value in this time as part of your writing life.

MOVEMENT AS SUSTENANCE FOR YOUR WRITING PRACTICE

RENÉE SAROJINI SAKLIKAR

"Let's write from a seated, cross-legged position," suggested the world-famous poet, a South Asian/American/English woman whom I admired.

My brain leapt at the chance to move but my legs folded into a lotus shape only with difficulty.

Around me, a group of fifteen writers, with our laptops and writing books: seated in the upstairs hallway outside a Gastown studio space. Outside, a cold November rain. Inside, my recalcitrant body, unused to the simple act of sitting cross-legged. That was seven years ago, and as I write these words, my fingers pause: although I'm in a dress, alone here in my pandemic office, I've taken two minutes to sit, cross-legged. Writing, particularly in precarious times, can lead us so deep into our heads that we disconnect from our bodies: posture, gait, flexibility, strength; these morph into distant concepts, and the more distant, the more our writing, sometimes, if we let it, can stagnate.

"The world wants you tight, stay loose" are words I once saw on a poster in the front entrance to an old bookstore on Columbia Street in New Westminster, the store, and indeed even the block of buildings in which it sat, long since demolished for condo towers.

The message, though, stays with me. And it's part of my invitation to you: consider movement an integral part of building your writing practice. Movement built into the practice of writing every day can help sustain your long-term writing goals and dreams.

When I wrote my first book, *children of air india: un/authorized exhibits and interjections* (Nightwood Editions, 2013), I stopped moving my body.

The work demanded deep focus. I sat surrounded by hundreds of documents. Sometimes, I found myself immobile for hours, listening to the voices of the dead. That labour took all my energy. I had nothing left. After a year of intense book promotion following publication, I was not only physically exhausted and out of shape, I was mentally exhausted too. Mercifully, I found my way out of non-movement and went on to re-engage with my body. And the key was listening to my stiff arms, tingling feet and sore legs, slack muscles, lungs that quickly ran out of breath: each one demanded I pay attention.

I started with small steps: walking and stretching; these lead me to yoga and eventually to dancing, and then to running. During this pandemic, I'm often back to just walking and stretching, but when I don't do even these things, my ability to write every day suffers.

You, also, might face writing work with demands that must be heeded to produce the story you need to share with the world. And these demands may drive you to sit for hours at your desk. So be it. All I'm suggesting is to keep a thread, loosely knotted, that ties you back to your body.

If you move your body enough as an accompaniment to your writing, you may be better able to realize your writing dreams and meet publication goals and deadlines. And you may then find that whether you are motivated to write, filled with the rush of a publication deadline, or in the doldrums of the "why bother blues," having a movement-based writing practice can keep you going.

Here are three suggestions for welcoming more movement into your writing practice:

Breathing: Sounds simple, and it is. And yet, I've observed that writers tend to breath shallowly when seated for hours in front of their screens. In fact, my unscientific and anecdotal observation is that when we sit for hours in front of screens, we forget to breathe!

If we shift that state by turning off our devices, we tend to find the space to breathe a bit more.

Prompt: Try this right now: put the book down or turn off your computer. Or, if that's not feasible, just look away from either your screen or your page. Move away from your phone. Look up, then down. Get your journal. Pick up a pencil or pen. Check in with yourself: are you breathing more? In my experience, when we consciously make time for micro-steps, we make the space for more profound change.

Pro-Tip: Try making time to unhook, unplug, and step away from your screen. Find a place other than your usual writing spot and walk to it. Maybe this will be a park bench or a condo courtyard or a blanket under that old beech tree you've been meaning to visit. Close your eyes, breathe in and out for three counts. Open your eyes, take hold of your pencil/pen, and begin. Simple. Try it right now.

Stretching: The internet will provide you with any number of ergonomic tips on how to incorporate ergonomic stretching into your writing day. Again, simple, easy, obvious. And yet, if on deadline, or engrossed in your story, how often do you take the time to stretch your arms, shake out your wrists, press your palms together, release?

Pro-Tip: Print out a diagram of your favourite office ergonomic stretches (you will find many on Pinterest), and pin your diagram just above your workstation. Try doing a set of these right now. And then try incorporating stretching every hour throughout the days you are writing.

Walking Meditation: In addition to stretching, I've incorporated walking meditation into my writing practice. It looks like this:

I try and write in my journal every morning (about one to three pages) and every evening, first thing before breakfast and last thing before bed. These pages are just free-flow thoughts. Often though, the flow of writing will unearth material for a scene or ideas for a new piece of writing. Once I've done my morning pages, I try and get outside for a walk in my neighbourhood. I set my timer for forty minutes: twenty minutes out, and twenty minutes back. If my work schedule doesn't allow for this, I at least walk for a minimum of twenty minutes. I do the same at dusk, either just before or just after my evening journal writing. The intent is to balance writing with walking in a seamless practice.

As I write, I find my writing tells me what I need to know, what I need to do.

For example, I've spent the last ten years working on an epic poem that combines verse and fiction techniques. For anyone reading this who is working on what I call "the long haul" — perhaps a novel, or a long poem, or a book of interconnected short stories — I encourage you to try the following "mantra/motto" exercise.

Pro-Tip: Try reflecting and then writing on the things you are truly focused on in your writing: themes, subjects, ideas, characters that continually crop up. You may find there's a pattern, a thought-process that reoccurs. From these, you might see that what you need to do is "create more space," or "find time to practice," or "write about Lucy." Each writer has their own thing, the thing that keeps you on the path to realizing your dream.

As part of this process, I've found it useful to think about what I call "mantra/mottos" for a set of months, even for a year. This year, prior to the pandemic, I wrote down, "stay inside the practice." Since COVID-19 hit us, that motto has morphed into this mantra: *Stay Inside The Story.*

During my morning, afternoon, and evening walks, I repeat this mantra — silently or just under my breath — as I walk. If I'm wearing a mask, it's easier to feel less self-conscious about chanting my mantra!

When I return to my busy day, I try and "stay close" to the feeling of the mantra and use it as a kind of shield to help me say no to inevitable distractions: texts, emails, social media, Zoom meetings, online chats, invitations to do things; and right now, during our pandemic, my urge to "doom-scroll": obsessively clicking on news sites and thumbing through Twitter.

Stay Inside The Story helps sustain my writing day.

Bonus Suggestion

Standing/Sitting Desk: One of the smartest investments I've made, thanks to a poetry prize, was to invest in a desk that moves up and down: from a seated position to standing, with adjustable heights. In addition to a regular office chair, I have a ball chair to go with the desk when it's at a "seated level." You will find many standing/sitting desks and lots of different chairs. Find the set up that works for you. Writing is tough on your body. Sustaining your writing practice means taking care of that body.

I wish every writer many blessings. Stay safe, keep writing. Find what sustains you. Shanti.

XRSS Renée Sarojini Saklikar

PROMPT:
Close your eyes. Reflect on this past week: what stands out for you? Open your eyes. Write one or two images/thoughts/ideas.

Close your eyes. Breathe. Listen to the sounds/silence around you. What do you hear?

Open your eyes. Write one or two things that you are hearing right now.

Try this simple micro-writing activity whenever you are about to begin your journal or your writing project.

GRAMMAR FOR WRITERS: IT'S NOT WHAT YOU THINK

REG JOHANSON

My "Grammar for Writers" workshop gets a couple of different responses. Some students are relieved that it wasn't what they thought it was going to be, that is, yet another opportunity to contemplate the supposed deficiencies in their use of language. Afterwards, they say they feel freer to experiment with their sentences. They find it liberating to see how sentences can be expanded, fragmented, unpunctuated, and brought closer to the multiple accents of everyday speech. The workshop affirms diversity, innovation, and pleasure in the way we speak and write.

On the other hand, some students are miffed that they didn't learn how to write correct sentences. They wanted me to go over common grammatical mistakes and give them tips on how to spot and correct them. Fair enough. There are good reasons for wanting that knowledge.

By "correct sentences," these students are referring to sentences like the ones I'm writing now. This is the syntax of what is known as Standard English. It's the form of English that our teachers correct us towards in school, the grammar (only one of many) that we learn the names for and the rules of. It's the form of English used in formal writing, which is most susceptible to standardization. Though it changes faster now, it is generally slower to change than other forms. New words and grammatical forms might be accepted as normal in speech and less formal writing for a long time before they begin to appear in Standard English.

The ability to reproduce Standard English is also highly prestigious. It may be a factor in decisions about who can enter as an immigrant, who gets good grades in school, who advances in a career. We make all sorts of conscious and unconscious racist and classist judgments about people based on the way they speak and write, as well as on their intelligence. Simply put, the closer a speaker/writer comes to Standard English, the more privilege they have.

Jila Ghomeshi, in her book *Grammar Matters: The Social Significance of How We Use Language*, makes a distinction between descriptive grammar and prescriptive grammar:

A descriptive grammar tells us about the form, meaning, and use [of language]. It tells us in what order the words must appear, the position of negation, the appropriate form of the pronoun, and the best choice of preposition. It provides phonetic information (how to pronounce the words) and semantic information (what the words mean). It describes all aspects of the sentences. A prescriptive grammar tells us something else: it tells us which one is better. It tells us that one sentence is correct and one is incorrect. That one is right and the other is wrong. It tells us not how language is used but how language ought to be used. Prescriptive grammars involve value judgments.[1]

The study of sociolinguistics — of how people actually use language, instead of how they ought to use language — doesn't talk about right and wrong or correct and incorrect. It's not interested in whether a way of speaking is "beautiful" or "ugly." Instead, usages are understood as standard or nonstandard, or, more to the point, stigmatized or prestigious.

This sociolinguistic perspective opens the crucial dimension of context. No rule is appropriate in all cases. Nothing is always correct. And beauty is, in fact, very much in the eye of the beholder. Writers need to have all the linguistic options open to them. It may be, for example, impossible for a writer to use Standard English at all. The community or character a novelist wants to represent may not speak that way. Poets may need to make interventions into standard grammar to reveal the assumptions and ideologies inherent in language, to make space for thinking in a new way. Standard English is nothing more than one rule-governed form of English among many, a form that happens to be aligned with power and privilege. When we speak or write it, we reproduce, and align ourselves with, that power and privilege. It's useful to be able to do that, but we don't always want to.

I often hear that we need to know the rules before we can break them. That's partially correct. If by "rules" we are only talking about the usual suspects among grammar errors (faulty parallelism, comma splice, dangling modifiers, etc.), there are many handbooks that go over common errors in Standard English. There is no shortage of resources available to writers who want to know how to fix common mistakes. More significantly, some attempts to write in dialect (i.e. nonstandard English), for example, devolve into caricature and stereotype because the writer doesn't know the rules of the speech community they are trying to reproduce.

On the other hand, our actual usage breaks the rules of Standard English all the time. That's why context is so important. Our ideas about what's acceptable change according to the who/where/what/how/why of the situation. Good writing adjusts to the rules of the context, not to the rules of the standard. Because a language is a living thing, the rules are always changing.

A text assumes a context. It assumes a specific readership and knows something about the expectations of that readership. A text inherits the legacy of all the texts like it, a literary history. There's no universal reader, and therefore no universal language. Sometimes the problem, especially for beginning writers, is that their knowledge of these contexts is limited or tacit. The more conscious of context — genre, history, audience — a writer is, the more effectively they'll be able to use the grammar that makes sense.

1. Jila Ghomeshi, *Grammar Matters: The Social Significance of How We Use Language* (ARP Books, 2010), pp.18-19

PROMPT:
Try any of the following: Experiment with expanding your sentences. Stack clause upon clause, adjective upon adjective. Follow a logic of digression through each sentence. Notice how, when you write this way, your sentences feel slow. They dwell and ruminate. For a good example, read *Absalom, Absalom!* by William Faulkner. This novel employs this sort of digressive, searching grammar as the means through which characters try, and fail, to understand their past.

Break up your sentences. Push the fragment. Writing in this way can convey irritation, impatience, frustration. For an example, you might read *Diamond Grill* by Fred Wah, in which this sort of grammar is used to express frustration with the demand to identify racially with one thing or another.

Write sentences that mimic the patterns and flow of speech. Beware of slipping into caricature or stereotype. A good example of this can be found in *Chelsea Girls* by Eileen Myles, in which the author reproduces the flow of a bar-room storyteller, full of digressions and interruptions.

Look through a piece of your own writing. What assumptions are you making in your use of punctuation about what's normal and what's deviant? Whose speech does your punctuation encode? Is it appropriate to your context? As an example, you might read the poem "low track" in *Mercenary English* by Mercedes Eng. In it, commas and apostrophes are mostly used in the places where we expect them in standard grammar, but the apostrophes that we might expect in words like "lookin," "beatin," and "lil" are refused. It's as if Eng is insisting that there is nothing missing at the end of "lookin" and "beatin" and in "lil." The apostrophes used in these cases in standard grammar indicate, of course, that letters are missing. But the letters are only missing according to the norms of standard pronunciation. For the speech community that Eng is encoding, nothing is lacking.

THE ART OF REREADING

KAYLA CZAGA

My go-to piece of advice for aspiring poets is: read! Read a lot. Read everything. I'm not unique in offering it. It's what my mentors and teachers told me to do. I imagine it's what their mentors and teachers told them to do. I've seen it on many advice lists from famous and successful writers. It feels like a no-brainer. Why would you even want to be a writer if you weren't an avid reader? That's like being a musician who doesn't listen to music. And yet I routinely mentor poets who don't read contemporary poetry.

There's this idea that the only requirement for being a poet is having strong thoughts and feelings, that poetry flows perfectly from one's soul — it can't be improved or taught, and it is independent of history or the world. I don't know where this idea comes from. When I was in grad school, my father mailed me a poem he'd written in rhymed quatrains that spoke in vague, symbolic language about a child who broke the mould set for them by their parents and teachers. When I talked to him on the phone about it, he suggested I try to get it published, that people would relate because it was his thoughts and feelings on paper. This was a man who had just watched me take four years of undergraduate courses in the field of poetry. If a genie ever granted me three wishes, I would spend one of them on eradicating the belief in the spontaneous and unteachable nature of poetry from the earth.

Poetry is happening now. Like all art, it exists in a continuum. It's influenced by what was written before it. There are schools and modes and chains of influence. So, I tell my students to read. Read things that were published in the last five years, the last three months. What I often forget to add: rereading may be equally important.

I moved to Vancouver in 2012 to attend the MFA program at the University of British Columbia. At that point, I had written several okay poems and had even published a few of them, but I didn't yet have what I would call my "voice." My poems always felt like improvisations, one-offs. During my undergrad, I drained recommended reading lists and rarely returned to the collections I'd finished, constantly moving on to the next suggestion.

Vancouver can be a nightmare to live in, especially if you don't have a lot of money. The summer before I was registered to take classes, I secured a bedroom in a basement suite with another student. It was affordable, but my bedroom didn't have any windows. I came with a twin mattress, a small dresser, and my stacks of books. There was a toddler living upstairs who suffered from night terrors, and almost nightly, I would wake to bottomless, primordial screams rippling through the ceiling followed by, "It's okay, Jacob. Jacob, you're okay. You're safe." Sometimes the screams started up again a little while later.

Among my stacks of books were a few volumes lent to me by my friend Jessie. She reads lots of literary magazines and usually has the first scoop on who's doing exciting things. (Another piece of advice I give to emerging poets: make friends with other writers.) One of these books was *Come On All You Ghosts* by Matthew Zapruder. I read the collection in a couple of afternoons. It's easy to do that with poetry. You can read a book in a day if you want to. If you've been feeling unproductive, I recommend reading a poetry book in an afternoon — it'll help. A week later, I decided to read the collection again because I wasn't sure if I liked it.

In that windowless room when I was twenty-two, the sensibilities of Zapruder's poems entered my writing brain and changed it. Later I would see the rhythms of Kenneth Koch, W.S. Merwin, and many others inside his poems, but at the time, Zapruder's voice was totally new to me, original. I reread the collection in order and then went back to my favourite poems. Then I reread my least favourite poems and asked myself why I didn't like them. Following the advice of one of my undergraduate instructors, Steven Price, who suggested I throw books I don't like across the room and never think about them again, I didn't linger long on these poems, just paused long enough to see if I'd missed any useful gems.

By the September I started my MFA, I had already read *Come On All You Ghosts* four or five times. That fall my poems started sounding the way I wanted my poems to sound. Looking back, I can see the influence of Zapruder in my word order and jumping between events. I can also see the influence of the windowless room: those poems are mostly set out of doors and have deep nostalgic tones. I wrote "Another Poem About my Father" and "That Great Burgundy-Upholstered Beacon of Dependability," two of the touchstone poems in my first book, a collection focused on family and coming of age. I didn't know they would become those poems or that I was even writing a book. I just had the sense I had finally started speaking as a poet.

Since then, I've continued to reread. I develop relationships with poems and whole collections. On each read, I notice something new. Sometimes I see the words and how they sound. Sometimes I see the architecture behind these sounds, the ways the poem hangs together. Rereading has taught me how to assemble my own poems.

The most useful habit that has developed out of my practice of rereading is the keeping of a poetry appreciation journal. I start by transcribing a poem I like into a notebook. Then I'll write down a few observations about the poem. Often my thoughts take point form — "Holy Volta Batman!" or "transitions," or "cool/creepy imagery" — but occasionally I'll write longer reflections, meditating on what a poem means to me. After my dad passed away in 2017, I decided to reread *Come On All You Ghosts*. On my first reading of the collection in 2012, mentions of the speaker's father's death hadn't stood out to me, but as I reread again, they appeared to dominate the collection.

Returning to *Come On All You Ghosts*, the collection that helped me establish my voice, has taught me how to write poems about grief. It has also helped me heal. I could reopen any of the books on my shelf that have meant something to me, and I would learn something new about poetry and about myself, my preoccupations, and what I care about right now in my writing journey. Rereading is the practice I return to most often, an act that nourishes, sustains, and deepens my craft.

PROMPT:
1. Write out by hand a poem that you enjoy.
2. If you are able to do so, read the poem out loud to yourself.
3. Spend a few minutes jotting down the things you appreciate about the poem. (If you get stuck, consider: its title, its lines and shape on the page, its figurative language, its images, its content, the ways its mind moves, its word choice, its sounds.)
4. Return to this poem several times over the next few hours or days, rereading it and making note of any new things you observe that you enjoy.
5. Pick one element from your list — ideally an element you'd like to improve in your own writing.
6. Use that element as a guide for your writing session. (For instance, if you like the sounds in a poem, spend some time making a list of words that use those sound devices in relation to a subject you're trying to write about; if you like the metaphors, break down the tenor and vehicle to better understand the connection being made; if you like the voice, look at the diction, noticing whether the sentences are long or short or both, whether the word choice is formal or more colloquial.)

MEMOIR IN THE EYE OF THE STORM

JOSEPH KAKWINOKANASUM

It was the summer of '78 when I knew someday, I'd be a writer. I was nine years old, and my sister gave me a paperback of short stories called *Night Shift* by Stephen King. I was inspired, and when I told my mother I wanted to be a writer, she said, "No such thing as an Indian writer."

I look more white than Native, but I am a card-holding member of the James Smith Cree Nation; I've always self-identified, but it rarely helped me in the small northern village where I grew up. Besides, having six siblings, five of them preceding me in school, made "passing" as white impossible. On the first day of class, some teacher would always ask, "How many more in your family are there?" After the class stopped laughing, I would answer, "Just one more." In grade school, I was transferred — along with the rest of the Native children — to the special needs group. I think it was the general assumption that Indians couldn't read, write, or count.

The establishment wasn't the only barrier I faced as an Indigenous writer. If you've had a childhood like mine, I'm truly sorry. If you're being subjected to abuse, extricate yourself from the scene. Get out. What writing has taught me is there are some stories that are worth seeking closure on; sure, I wouldn't change a thing about what I lived through, but do I want to live it over? Nope. I wound up having a nervous breakdown and found myself at St. Paul's Hospital in the psych ward. It's how I met my therapist.

Therapy helped me work through my anxiety, fears, and trauma and put me on a more self-aware path. It was my therapist who suggested journaling as a catharsis, and twenty years of that led me to reconcile with my past and prepare me for the future. I still have bad days, but I have a protocol for such events that makes dealing with my depression, chronic pain, and concussion syndrome easier. I continue to work with my therapists. That's right, therapists, plural. I have a backup just in case. I even have an amazing family physician who is Native, and all my doctors know my story. At first therapy was difficult because I struggled with my past, but now I have healthier habits than I did when I was an addict. That's right! Not ashamed. I'm lucky I lived through the experience. Through therapy, I've come to an understanding of my relationship with addiction, developed a personal relationship with my triggers, and learned how to deal with them safely.

There is a lot to say about lived experience, and Natives are acutely aware of social obstacles like poverty, abuse addiction, and a society that is just now learning about institutionalised racism and its own privilege. Of all the challenges I faced as an Indigenous person, the hardest has been reprograming the hardwired lessons beat into me as a child. "You stupid fucking Indian" was the most repeated message I recall growing up. I spent years looking back, wondering why, questioning, always doubting myself. I had no self-confidence.

A difficult childhood and growing up dirt poor may sound like a bad start to a writing career, but it can also be dangerous, especially if you are Native; and if I wanted to be a writer, I needed help. Therapy and journaling were my first steps to healing, even if I didn't know it at the time. I stumbled constantly along a path toward inner peace, where I eventually discovered the validation to unpack my ambitions of being a writer. While in therapy, I took writing courses; I read Natalie Goldberg's *Writing Down the Bones: Freeing the Writer Within* and Stephen King's *On Writing: A Memoir of the Craft*. I wrote daily, built a box for my writing tools, spent all my spare money on postage, stationery, and the like. As bad as the writing was, I submitted it anyways. Then one summer day in 2014, I got an email that reminded me of a longshot application I had submitted with the help of a good friend. I read the message: "Congratulations Joseph!" I had won the Canada Council for the Arts creation grant for aboriginal peoples, writers, and storytellers.

In 2015 I read the Truth and Reconciliation Commission of Canada's (TRC) findings and learned why growing up in my family was so difficult. The TRC gave exigence to indigenous stories. It's no secret to us Native people that the unpleasant experience of childhood is mostly mutual and eerily similar. There were times I was so enveloped by the TRC I became seriously depressed. To this day a critic sits on my shoulder gorging on my self-esteem, washing it down with my spirit. As an Indigenous writer, I have learned to work away from that voice until I can't hear it. I have given a lot of time and effort to create a safe space and support system to be a writer, and knowing when to pull away from the writing is as important a tool as knowing when to get back to it. It's hard to put it into just a few words, especially when you are in the throes of it and up to your neck in your manuscript, so it is important to write from a safe place, and to rest from the difficult work that is memoir writing.

When I write memoir, I know that there are inherent risks to the practice. I know that I need to take it slowly. I write for ten or fifteen minutes, stop, then I get up from my desk and go for a walk, or I do house chores, or play with my cats. This is more a grounding exercise than anything; I have to physically remind myself to remain grounded and in the present moment, or I risk being pulled down by the gravity of my trauma. That said, I've learned that bad days are a part of my creative process, and if I find myself spiralling into a darkness, I call my therapist, talk to my closest friends, and meditate. If I am still struggling, I go to bed. Seriously, I sleep. If it's good enough for the Dalai Lama, it's good enough for me. Rest is the best, and it's important to remember that life is a practice and not a perfect.

Writing takes a lot of work, so I encourage all new writers to get involved in a writer's group and even create your own group of readers who are willing to review your writing. I attended the Writer's Studio (TWS), offered through Simon Fraser University, where I made some good writer friends who continue to inspire and support me daily. A good friend from TWS once said to me, "Joseph, you are not your writing." And he was right. This statement is a reminder of where I started and that my past has less impact on my process. This is why I don't throw away my journals, because if I want to, I can grab any one of them, and see how I have evolved as a writer and as a human being.

The writing experience has allowed me to refine and sharpen my writing tools. Over the years, I have collected a shed full of tools that I use to tend the enormous manure heap that was my childhood. I've broken that ground with blood, sweat, and tears, tilled it into a rich garden until my hands bled. I tend my garden almost daily, and sometimes I have to mend it. From that garden, I've learned, through trial and error, what is good for me and what makes me sick with anxiety, fear, and bitter sadness; and although my mother's voice continues to resonate, she is not saying, "no such thing as an Indian writer."

PROMPT:
1. Set up your writing station so that you won't need to get up from your chair. You'll need a journal and pen. Coffee is optional.
2. Open your journal to a blank page, and write a list of ten words that describe how you are currently feeling. The words can be broad (happy, sad, angry) or more specific (defiant, flummoxed, jittery). Contradictory words are encouraged — we are so rarely feeling only one thing.
3. Choose your two favourite words from your list.
4. Set a timer for half an hour, and write about where these two feelings come from. Is this a feeling brought on by a specific set of circumstances? Something you feel regularly? Do you know why you are feeling the way you do, or will you need to dig deeper to figure it out?

WRITE YOUR GRAIN OF SAND

PETER BABIAK

Like many students who set out to study language and literature, I was initially drawn to the Romantic poets. To William Wordsworth, Samuel Taylor Coleridge, and, in particular, William Blake, whose written work and engravings were so prophetic and revolutionary in spirit, yet so strikingly simple, that they threw open new doors of perception for me. As a student, and then a teacher, of literature and linguistics, it was enough for me to understand the content of Blake's work, to theorize it, or discuss it academically. Over the years, however, as I gradually and uncomfortably started to consider myself a creative essayist, a writer — a designation I still only use hesitantly — I found that Blake's work helped me structure my own narratives and the writing of the students I teach. Let me explain.

Here are the opening lines of Blake's "Auguries of Innocence," which I often put on screen the first day of my creative non-fiction class. The lines are so often quoted, that many people are familiar with the sentiment, even if they've never read the poem:

> To see a World in a Grain of Sand
> And a Heaven in a Wild Flower
> Hold Infinity in the palm of your hand
> And Eternity in an hour

Take a deep dive into the nature of the smallest details, Blake seems to say in each of these lines that partner universals with particulars, and you'll see, slowly and by degrees, a world unfold before your eyes. It's a good message for everybody, but it's especially helpful to students who've convinced themselves — as many do, just as I did — that their experiences are not interesting enough to write about. Wrong, I say. Some of the most muscular writing is about what we often think of as insignificant minutiae.

Consider, for example, these classic literary works about mundane activities and situations. Xavier de Maistre's classic *Voyage Around My Room*, a travel memoir about the author's room, was written while he was under a month's house arrest for dueling, a story particularly fitting for the COVID-19 era of home-bound living. Joan Didion's *Slouching Towards Bethlehem*, a landmark in creative non-fiction, was written about a small countercultural neighbourhood in San Francisco. Anthony Bourdain's *Kitchen Confidential: Adventures in the Culinary Underbelly* is a zesty memoir about the life of a chef that takes its inspiration from a behind-the-restaurant scene the author had the good fortune to witness first hand. Or one of my favourites, by the master author of ordinariness, Nicholson Baker, *A Box of Matches* centres on a man who wakes up every morning before sunrise, makes coffee, checks in on his duck, then, before his wife wakes up, just thinks about life in all its granular richness, rendering the elementary particles into literary sublimity, even though the narrative never moves beyond his home.

Every writer, especially those new to the craft, should be reminded that a life doesn't happen in grand narratives. Look to the smallest moments, the minutiae that seem profoundly unliterary, and you might find that it can deliver the universe of an entire story. Folding laundry or doing the dishes and looking out the window and wondering what the neighbours are building in their garage. That time you walked to the restroom at Darby's and overheard the woman telling her boyfriend or husband "if you don't like my peaches" but nothing else.

Managing your micro-experience, extrapolating from the grain of sand, is a matter of crafting sentences, the elementary particles all stories need. To that end, the first assignment I give when I teach creative non-fiction is to have students bring an example of a sentence they "love." One sentence. It could be from anywhere — novel, poem, song, even a textbook — but it must be a sentence they find memorable because it provokes a thought or carves an image. I'll put up an example on the screen, something like Dickens's sixty-word opening to *A Tale of Two Cities* — "It was the best of times, it was the worst of times…" — and then explain that I find it memorable, not because the narrative is about the French Revolution, but because of its *written-ness*. That series of repeated clauses draws me in because it organizes contrasting points into tight, successive clauses, which produce a memorable cadence. Then, with my example — and in the next class, too, with their own examples — I write the sentence on the board, but leave out the nouns and verbs, then I ask the students to fill in the blanks. A few will complain that this sounds too much like a grammar exercise, that parsing a sentence is not what they had in mind when they signed on for creative non-fiction.

What we're actually doing here, I'll say, is learning how to build sentences by modelling them on the architecture of other sentences. The lesson aims to illustrate that language isn't a neutral mechanism, a release valve that lets you express various lived experiences and perceptions. To the extent that every writer wants to be read, they must convince themselves that readers will only ever experience their words and sentences, not the experiences themselves. In creative non-fiction, the world that you are supposed to be writing about isn't just "out there" waiting to be told. It's produced in your telling, much like history follows the laws of storytelling, rather than being a set of chronicled empirical events.

This leads to the next step, which is to pivot from single sentences to an entire narrative. To make the transition, I resort to a principle of language theory and say, following the French writer Roland Barthes, "there is nothing in discourse that is not to be found in a sentence," which is another way of saying that an individual sentence (built with nouns and verbs) is the microcosm for an entire narrative (built with characters and time) and that leads back to Blake's grain of sand.

Take a single event or episode from your life, something small or anecdotal, and let it be the carrying vessel for your story. Begin by asking what thought that event led to, and then — crucially — say how that thought came about. How did looking out the window while washing dishes lead you to an exposition on the ethics of suburban neighbours? That time you overheard the woman say that thing about peaches, how did your girlfriend react when you told her, and what led to the two of you engaging in a slightly antagonistic discussion of sexist metaphors?

It always helps to secure relatively abstract conversations about narrative structure with concrete experience. I've said that I hesitate to call myself a "writer," a creative essayist, and that's still true today because I had convinced myself that nothing I wrote would be interesting to readers. For years I plugged away, writing essays that were a blend of memoir and cultural commentary. But about a decade into my writing sub-career, I experienced the good fortune of having a few of my essays nominated for provincial and national magazine awards, and a couple were anthologized in the annual Best Canadian Essays series. The element each of my essays had in common, is that they were all based on confined experiences. A phone message from a friend I'd lost touch with who called to ask "Are you happy?" became the vessel for an expository memoir on how the modern world enforces a kind of happiness on us and why this isn't such a good thing. An afternoon watching students play *Pokémon Go* became an essay on technology, inflected with detours into how factual history is shaped by literary tools like metaphor and characterization.

There are two more examples that illustrate how I found an entire story by protracting the granular particles of my own experience into literary events. The first, which lasted a mere twenty seconds, was a trip down the escalators at Metrotown mall when, quite suddenly, I regained my sense of smell after years of anosmia. Granted, a reawakened sense of smell is no small event, but that essay was more about how we contort words to signify visceral experiences. The descent offered a built-in narrative frame with a beginning, middle, and end;

the clunky movements, punctuated by patterned reverberations of the escalator's motor, offered repeated intervals where I could pause, shift out of real-time, and detour into musing on the distinct behaviour of people in malls, and even move into cerebral considerations of why we can only resort to the universal simile "it's like" when describing scents, or taste, or any other sensory experience, for that matter. The second episode, equally pedestrian, but more grim, was the excruciating hour or so it took me to drive the ten kilometres back home after learning that my wife had suffered a heart attack. As much as I avoided thinking about that tragic day, I found that when I did revisit it, the story just wouldn't stay on my wife's death; it kept veering towards therapeutic vignettes on family, expositions on friendship, and the enchanted thinking which death delivers to us all.

I tell my students the organizing event of their narrative can be unassuming, or just small and confined, but it might work best if it is protracted, interrupted with anecdotes and recollected dialogue, infused with reflections or speculations — historical, academic, personal — and generally written about with an eye to expressing the event's literariness. It's not the only way to write narrative, of course, but it is an effective approach, certainly for me. I hope, too, that this has helped my students write better. In many cases, I think it has. I've received: an essay by a young woman who spent a summer working with her dad framing houses; a poignant piece on a Saturday golf game by a young man who wrote it as a beautiful homage to his father, who had apparently taught him how to play but for some reason was no longer a regular part of the man's life; an essay by a woman who was daunted with the prospect of returning to school but overcame it by, of all things, trying out for a roller derby team in Vancouver; another by a student who ate from dumpsters outside the restaurants on Commercial Drive, between First and Venables, just to share the experiences of homeless people and dumpster divers known as "fregans." Each of these essays is an attempt to find a world in a single grain of sand; in each, an inconspicuous experience is recast as a memorable, literary event.

PROMPT:

Think of an event or experience that appears, at first glance, unremarkable and profoundly unliterary. Write it down in note form, but include dates, times, and any other contextual information. It could be *any*thing, like looking out the kitchen window while doing dishes or overhearing snippets of conversation. To extrapolate from your granular experience, ask yourself, first, what two or three thoughts or ideas it evokes in you, both then and now? Document them. Then, second, ask yourself specifically *how* those thoughts and ideas (or anecdotes, arguments, narratives, opinions, parallel events, etc.) came about? Document them. Choose one of these thoughts and use it as a basis for a mini-essay where you write a story about your insignificant event or experience but make it significant by extrapolating and writing more meaningfully about the thoughts and ideas it provokes.

THE FAMILIAR IN THE FAMILIAR ESSAY

JOHN WHATLEY

[The] mind in creation is as a fading coal, which some invisible influence, like an inconstant wind, awakens to transitory brightness; this power arises from within [...][1] — Percy Bysshe Shelley

So here I am now, quite a lot older, and becoming inured to being locked down at home during the COVID-19 crisis. One of the things I'm allowed, is to walk around my neighbourhood with my wife Laurel and our Belgian Malinois, Sage, something I've not done continuously before my retirement and COVID-19. After twenty-five years, I yet feel like oil on water here, no belonging, no great record of mixing with all the families that live here and around me, though I know a few. Now, though, after a steady year of this walk, sometimes three per day, I think I know every crack and cranny, bush, root, branch, foundation, roof, gutter, window, and some of the more defensive dogs. The feeling of being part of it, of being familiar with it, now comes in bits and pieces, mixed in, though, with being a stranger. I think I'm learning all the usual ways of recognition, but it's not a smooth continuous feeling of entering a place I deeply know. Betwixt and between, we walk up street A two blocks, east across 28th to street G, down three blocks to 25th, one long block west next to Highway 1 — about thirty feet below — where we hear the slip and flow of traffic, the swiftness of its passing in relation to our plodding, as we rewrite this line again. I imagine the other side of the highway fence as a slipstream of coolly passing, hidden, jet aircraft, while the familiar houses, windows, garden hedges, fences, dogs, and sidewalks above remain steady, in place, defining stability, perhaps something like continuity, perhaps familiar.

My dog is a beautiful animal. And he also inscribes a line between the strange and the familiar, distinguishing himself from all the other dogs, knowing all of them and now quite used to their odorous languages, local idioms, and, for those trapped inside, their muted cacophony as he passes, and he's ready for any new insurgency anywhere. For us though, unlike his warrior pedigree, the line we inscribe likely comes from the fact that I immigrated to Canada in the '70s, have worked at a local university for over twenty-five years, and have recently returned to civilian life, and no one else here, or very few, know what I do or have done in any detail. The major difference I can find, is that I write, teach writing and critical reading, and have likely read and corrected about eight thousand student essays. It is conceivable that my neighbours also grade papers or write on gardening, flying, or bees, though I imagine the number who write familiar essays is few.

There are useful differences between writing a university essay and a familiar essay. The critical essay is not allowed to use the "I" pronoun, while the familiar revels in it. The formal essay logically unfolds to a conclusion or marshals support for a claim, while the familiar is digressive, only includes expertise when called for, but never reaches certainty, only a glimpse, a provisional understanding or insight, always up for revision. The etymology of the French "essai" is close to an "assay," the sifting and testing of an ore for its value. But there is no final definition of either type. In his *A Dictionary of the English Language* (1755), Samuel Johnson might have grumpily called the essay "A loose sally of the mind; an irregular, undigested piece," but he wrote some superbly crafted literary essays himself, clearly recognizing their aesthetic, disciplinary, and persuasive possibilities. While he may have begun the modern, academic essay with its lumber of a "review of the literature" — its logical development and its extensive erudition — all of his essays on Shakespeare, Savage, Pope, Young, and others, have a familiar undertone, a feeling for both place and loss of place and aloneness. Interesting that we do not allow any note of familiarity like this in the university essay. And, on the other side, the originator of the familiar essay, Michel de Montaigne, discovered the *essai* while retired in the 1590s in his chateau near Bordeaux during a raging religious war and hoped it would bring back the familiar. In "Of Vanity," (1590s) he said, "there should be some restraint of law against foolish and impertinent scribblers, as well as against vagabonds and idle persons; which if there were, both I and a hundred others would be banished from the reach of our people." There it is. As Montaigne lets us know, we begin nowhere, as idle vagabonds. Writing a familiar essay, one begins in paradox, without feeling part of anything in the world, anywhere.

In my neighbourhood, I'd like to think that, like Montaigne, here and there I do share something, though it is not belonging; and it certainly isn't a continuous sense of being in *my* place, or of commitment to the people in *my* neighbourhood. No that's not it. I'm a baby boomer. I've lived all over the place. So, less like Johnson, and more like Dickens's "Night Walks" (1860), where, unable to sleep, he tallies up his forays into night-time London as a "houseless" person, comparing himself with the others he meets, in doorways, and those on the graveyard shift of London's market workers. Or of Didion's "On Going Home," where she takes the risk of entering into a depth analysis of what it was like going back to her home in rural California after marriage, and trying to explain the difference to her new husband and daughter. Or of Angelou's "Graduation," and the difficulties of being a Black high school student in Georgia and being promised certain vocations in the graduation speech by the superintendent. Identification, but alienation and difficulty as well. Gutkind's phrase "true stories well told" might be close, but while he includes the skills of narrative, the reach to include the familiar in itself is missing in his brief.

The familiar essay and its voice, though, is everywhere in the magazine universe. You see it in the bylines and reviews of *The Economist*, in *The New Yorker*, in *Maclean's*, in creative non-fiction, or in a story by Leslie Jamison in *Harper's* (2015), which deals with the story of a child (Leininger) convinced he was the reincarnation of a World War II fighter pilot shot down in the Pacific. Jamison's narrative includes all the personal pronouns; she is absorbed by the story, visits all the players, and ends with her own evaluation:

Did I leave feeling that the Leiningers were sincere in their beliefs about reincarnation? Absolutely. [...] It seemed to me that they were just a family seeking meaning in their experience, as we all do. In this case, the human hunger for narrative — a hunger I experience constantly, and from which I make my living — had built an intricate and self-sustaining story, all of it anchored by the desire to care for a little boy in the dark.[2]

A story, then, that becomes interesting as it is progressively engaged in by the narrator herself. There is attention to science, objectivity, and disciplined research, but finally, the realization that the familiar itself must become the focus and theme.

For the narrative of my neighbourhood, with which I began, there may never be any long term or depth familiarity. I've no family here. Nothing like the upcountry connections that many of my neighbours have: connections to mothers, fathers, children, brothers, sisters, uncles, and aunts working in the forest industry, or for BC Hydro, or one of the ski resorts, or having retired, say, to Kelowna. Nothing like seventy years of life lived in one place.

Thus, if there is one goal of the familiar essay: it is simply to find the familiar. Some of our neighbours do recognize us, and we them; one family we know quite well lives there, in a small house we pass to the left as we swing onto 28th. He's an artist; she was a finance executive, now retired. And he has a smaller dog that mine just tolerates. But my dog is exceptionally testy around other dogs, so we are too, and worried about the singletons or couples who also have them on their leashes or get them on as soon as we show up. We likely have that uncertain reputation of owning a testy dog. But we've made connections. And there are streets above ours which I'm in awe of—because they so strongly indicate familiarity, neighbourhood, belonging. Something about the way the houses have been there for at least sixty or seventy years, Queen Anne-like. Back to the time North Vancouver was a shipbuilding town in World War II; old fashioned, three-storey homes, some beautifully renovated and painted, some in deep disrepair; all, though, individuals, their self-presentation projecting their owners' states perfectly with a complex, almost abstract fitting of each to the other down the whole block. The lines of familiarity and strangeness are maintained with artistic precision front, back, and sides and meticulously maintained. And at the end of 28th that small dump truck, often full of a day's worth of collecting, ready for the transfer station; perhaps that's the way that last family on the block survives? During the summer, next to his fence with a lawn mower, he is friendly and talks to us about dogs and gardening as we pass by. Their fitting is so close we are being included. And that house further down by the highway, with a white, older pick-up seriously full of metal junk — water heaters, scrap iron, rusted auto wheels, brakes, other metal bits of building debris — and the man who makes his living by collecting and reselling it. The house needs paint. After a number of years, a huff of recognition as we pass. I have the feeling that these two collectors, three blocks apart, have been there for years, and are the deeper part of the history of the neighbourhood, aging in place, collecting their particular pieces of it. They are deeply in tune with the familiar, though a familiar gradually slipping away into "the transfer station" or scrap yard.

Maybe, after all, this place is no longer just a backdrop for the sudden forward motion of going to work, the turn of the car down the street to get to the highway, the daily passing by and exit from a bedroom community, maybe it *is* the thing itself. The familiar, the North Star.

1. Percy Bysshe Shelley, "A Defence of Poetry." 1821, 1840.

2. Leslie Jamison, "Giving up the Ghost: The eternal allure of life after death," *Harper's Magazine*, March, 2015.

PROMPT:

The essay above is designed to help you recognize and begin to write the familiar essay. You can, as with most of the literary arts today, begin anywhere about anything and everything. The familiar is, after all, what is most close to you. It is the easiest of entrances, the gateway to everywhere around you, all those surfaces, all those perceptions and memories so close to hand. It is often the closest prose gets to poetry. There can be a randomness at its beginning: select what you want to select, where your fingers itch. And once you start, you'll realize how complex the surfaces are around you, and you'll want to capture some of them just in themselves. They become, in this alive space of the familiar, suddenly interesting. Follow your own reasons, put others on hold for later in the essay. Focus on that quick hummingbird, that way in which the light shines on a mirror edge. Whatever. Two opposing views on what you are after: "It is not easy to write a familiar style. Many people mistake a familiar for a vulgar style, and suppose that to write without affectation is to write at random. On the contrary, there is nothing that requires more precision, and, if I may so say, purity of expression [...]" ("On Familiar Style" from *Table Talk, Essays on Men and Manners* by William Hazlitt, 1822). And then David Shields from his 2010 *Reality Hunger: A Manifesto*: "An artistic movement, albeit an organic and as-yet-unstated one, is forming. What are its key components? [...] Randomness, openness to accident and serendipity, spontaneity, artistic risk, emotional urgency and intensity [...] a blurring (to the point of invisibility) of any distinction between fiction and non-fiction: the lure and blur of the real"[3]. And, finally, you are the one who must put these two together, the random and the precise, accident and shaping, the blur and its capture: the poem at the centre of your familiar essay.

3. David Shields, *Reality Hunger: A Manifesto* (Vintage Books, 2011), 5.

FOR MEMOIRISTS

JJ LEE

While the techniques that follow may help writers of memoir engage with difficult or elusive memories, they are in no way a replacement for therapy, or the medically proven methods used to treat trauma or disorders stemming from it.

There are all sorts of reasons you, the memoirist, may be prevented from being able to recall a memory. You may have experienced the event at too young an age. The event may have been too traumatic. The event may not have felt important at the time, and now you plain forget. Or maybe you have retold the tale too many times, and it has ossified in the mind.

Regardless of the reasons, it is difficult to write well about the past when the details are scant or flat. It's even worse to have to recount a tale that offers no surprise or insight for the teller. I say, "no surprise for the writer leads to no surprise for the reader." And writing about something that is dead cold and without freshness or colour is just a horrible chore.

To bring a memory back to life, I encourage the memoirists to employ a remembering exercise I call "The Fly." It's a guided tour through a past experience that entails a certain mindset and specific techniques of recall that have proven, time and time again, to unlock the literary potential of a specific memory. Here's how it works.

1. *Understand you are not you.* You are a *writer* who creates a *narrator* on the page that recounts the story of a *main character* in the first person. The distinction is important for a number of reasons. It allows you to have psychological distance from the person who experienced the event. You may say, "Isn't that me?" But, of course, you aren't, not anymore. You, the writer, are older, wiser, and possess more perspective on the past event than the person who originally experienced the event.

   This approach is particularly helpful if you are grappling with a traumatic memory. Often remembering a painful past can retraumatize you. One way this happens is you fall into reliving the event as the past self. In other words, when you recall, you revert to an earlier version of yourself and forgo the insight, maturity, and strength you may now possess. So, imagine yourself as the *writer*.

2. *Put on your armour.* It may seem contradictory to put on emotional armour when you're trying to re-engage more deeply with a semi-lost memory but think of deep-sea explorers. To reach the bottom of the ocean and uncover its mysteries, you need a submarine with a strong hull. I have advised writers to imagine themselves climbing into an imaginary vehicle (for example, ahem, a steel fly).

3. *Dive, dive, dive.* Don't think of the memory as an event but as a single space, like a stage set. Get inside your steel fly or teeny-tiny submarine, and float down into the memory space. Make it devoid of any characters, including the main character. Describe a single detail in the setting, like a chair, and then describe the objects next to it and so on until a good portion is recreated in your mind and on the page. If you have troubling remembering, this portion of the exercise really works.

4. *Enter main character.* Remain in your vessel. Imagine your earlier self, the main character, entering the space. Observe this person from a distance and an angle slightly above. This helps with psychological

distance. Provide a character sketch. What are they wearing exactly? How do they look? Try to avoid being judgmental. Have some empathy and observe them the way you would a stranger passing you on the street.

5. *Enter the rest of the cast.* Bring the other relevant characters into the space. Don't make them do anything. Just describe them one by one, as you did for the main character.

6. *Set the memory in motion.* It is important for you to remain inside the metaphorical vessel. See the main character as external to you. Start the action. What are people doing and saying? Write it all down.

   For dialogue, record what you recall people saying. Note: it's different from quoting in a news or magazine article. Memoir is a record of remembering. What was said is how you recall it. It is not an exact record, and that's fine, as long as this particular approach to dialogue is properly acknowledged in the text where possible.

   For action, break it down into the smallest possible meaningful unit (advances plot, tracks character change, etc.). So, in a dull memoir, the tale may go: "In three months, we restored the old black Comet so we could cycle to town and back." Action, broken down, could read, "The first two days in the shed, I stripped the frame of paint. My son wouldn't look up from his smart phone. On the third, I donned a mask and pulled out a can of gold enamel spray. He couldn't resist." Crude, I know. You get the point.

7. *Credo and motivation.* Credo is a belief that drives character action. An example would be, "the main character believes nobody loves him." Motivation is the goal of character action. So, then, the action may be hitting on potential partners, but the motivation is, "he constantly seeks to be dating someone without interruption."

   Give a reason and a goal for the action and dialogue in your story. Why does the main character do what they do? What underlying belief informs the motivation and action? It's the most important part of the tale. It gives the memory weight. It also provides a window for the writer to examine the main character like a fictional character. It can be enlightening.

8. *More credo and motivation.* Take your vessel and float around the other characters. Look at them. Use your people sense. What do they believe? What do they want to achieve? What makes them do what they do?

    For memoirists who have suffered trauma, this might be the hardest thing with which they will grapple. This struggle to understand or have insight can be rewarding, but it is fraught. My advice in such cases is, the hotter the emotion or feelings about a memory, the cooler the writer and the narrator needs to be. It gives you the space you need to get through the task.

9. *Messages in a bottle.* Begin to surface from the memory. As you rise above it all, answer two final questions: what would the main character want to tell the writer; and what would the writer want to tell the main character?

    You may be surprised what they have to say to each other.

DANGEROUS TERRITORIES: ON WRITING AND RISK

LEANNE DUNIC

I was nineteen when I picked up a copy of *The Jade Peony* by Wayson Choy for twenty-five cents at a library book sale. Before that, I didn't know that anyone cared to publish Chinese Canadian stories and was so happy to be proven wrong. If I hadn't stumbled upon this book then, who knows how much longer it would've been before I recognized that stories by people like me were desirable?

The Jade Peony started as a short story written while Choy was the first Chinese Canadian student enrolled in a creative writing class at the University of British Columbia. It was published in its novel form in 1995 — a time when it was unheard of to have a book in which the main characters were Asian. Choy's risk was our community's gain. He was one of the first openly gay writers of colour and broke ground for Chinese Canadian and minority voices struggling to have their work taken seriously in a white, heteronormative literary landscape.

Choy would go on to write more award-winning books. About writing, he said, "You have to risk everything to make a breakthrough." As readers, we are compelled by Choy's bold depictions of histories and experiences, as well as his complex and authentic characters. For many readers, this material felt new, and to others, like myself, it was refreshingly familiar. Choy's writing was also controversial in the Chinese Canadian community, as depictions of community stories, and of Chinese Canadian queerness, had not been normalized.

One could argue that there is still a lot of work to do in regards to the latter.

Since the publication of *The Jade Peony*, Asian Canadian writers continue to make their mark on the country's literary scene. One such voice is Kim Thúy, a Vietnamese-born Canadian writer. Originally published in French, her debut novel, *Ru*, is a poetic take on her experience of being a Vietnamese refugee.

The book was controversial in Vietnam, which had not formally acknowledged the boat people crisis in their history books. Thúy's book served as a portal of knowledge for the unknowing generations of people born after the event.

The epigraph of the book states:

In French, ru means a small stream, and, figuratively,
a flow, a discharge — of tears, of blood, of money.
In Vietnamese, ru means a lullaby, to lull.

This passage clues the reader into how to read the book. The novel's form is atypical, compiled with lyrical vignettes that read lightly like a lullaby, the struggles of her characters flowing on the page. The form serves the story with its use of space and page breaks. As Jane Alison writes in her book *Meander, Spiral, Explode: Design and Pattern in Narrative*, "Rather than expecting the 'soul' or animating shape of fiction to be a plotted arc, why not imagine shapes?"

Thúy continued to use this form for her book *Mãn*, which uses Vietnamese words in the margins to anchor each vignette. In the passage "đắng/bitter," Thúy opens with the protagonist helping her husband convalesce by "gently cooking chicken with lotus seeds, ginkgo nuts and dried goji berries," a description that evokes not only flavours and aromas, but memories and emotion. The text is as redolent as the protagonist's cooking. Even the book's title, *Mãn*, works on multiple layers, as it's the protagonist's name, the word for "fulfillment" in Vietnamese, and, of course, bears a resemblance to a word in English. Thúy's books are rich with layered symbolism.

These are just two examples of literary risks — risks with form, and with content. The efforts of these authors inspired generations of writers to follow them, and advanced representation in Canadian literature. These authors, and others like them, gave me the validation that my stories might matter, too.

I started writing in earnest a decade ago with an idea for a novel. A few years later, that novel morphed into a collection of poems, and later, a lyric memoir. Inspired by the risk-taking of authors like Choy and Thúy, I made myself vulnerable by writing about intimate relationships without the curtain of fiction while using non-linear fragments. Ten years after coming up with the initial concept for the work, the manuscript finally found its final shape and a home with Talonbooks.

The previous iterations of the book, while they may have felt like failures at the time, were essential to my process. And isn't that true in life, too? That we need to fail in order to really learn? We can either exploit all the things which are comfortable and safe, or we can explore dangerous territories. What are you afraid of writing about? What would happen if you threw caution to the wind and committed to writing about it? How can you challenge norms for the better? How can you approach your work in a way that excites both you and the reader? How can you be inspired in ways to refresh your work?

I wrote this essay while listening to Tchaikovsky's Piano Concerto No. 1. The piece opens with a brash announcement from the horn section, followed by three bold and resonant piano chords that move as slow triplets along the full spread of the keys. I imagined this essay's structure as those three piano chords. I don't know if my experiment of essay-mimicking-Tchaikovsky worked, but it got me here. I'm excited to cheer you on with your experiments and risk-taking, your growth in becoming a better writer and human.

PROMPT:

Write a response to a piece of music that you find challenging to listen to (suggestions: Stravinsky's The Rite of Spring; John Coltrane's *Ascension*; Emerson, Lake & Palmer's *Tarkus*; or Billy Ray Cyrus's "Achy Breaky Heart"). Experiment with content and/or form. Bonus points for shaking up your writing materials!

WRITING FROM THE EDGES: WE ARE SO MUCH MORE THAN OUR CIRCUMSTANCES

JÓNÍNA KIRTON

Just as a bird soars on two wings, a seeker is liberated through self-effort and grace.
— Gurumayi Chidvilasananda

As writers, we are seekers. Whether or not we view this in a spiritual context, writing is not just something we do. For most of us, it is a calling: one that requires self-effort and grace. Self-effort is encouraged and rewarded in many things and, no doubt, has a place in your writing life, but all the effort in the world cannot replace what grace brings to the page. Grace has many names, including synchronicity, luck, the muse, and Spirit, to name a few. She is most attracted to those who see and feel her, especially those who give thanks for her assistance. Many rely too heavily on self-effort, forgetting that grace is available to them.

More on grace later. Let's start with self-effort and the many practical things you can do to make writing well a reality.

As students of a writing life, we are offered advice like that of Virginia Woolf, who once said, "A woman must have money and a room of her own if she is to write [...]" This kind of advice, while good, can be discouraging to those who do not have the means required for an extra room or to quit their job. Some emerging writers are writing from the edges of things. They are not well resourced. Even though there has been a huge push for inclusion, much of it has ignored or downplayed the financial disparities that exist in the writing world. In fact, too often the above quote is shortened to simply say that a woman "needs a room of her own," as if that is all that one needs. The good news is that writing is one of the most accessible art forms one can undertake. All you really need is a pen and some paper. That is, of course, unless you have need of specialized technical support, so require a computer. In that case, there may be grants available so that you can purchase the equipment you need. A room of one's own is not essential, especially if you can create "a room of your own" in your mind. The "support" can come from a writing group and need not have any costs attached to it. If we can't attend classes or workshops, there are libraries with countless books on writing, some offered in audio form. Authors like Richard Wagamese simply read extensively, and he became an award-winning prolific writer. When I was in circle with him, he spoke of his frequent visits to local libraries, during times when he was homeless and had nothing. What he did have, was the call to write. One could say his gift was calling him. As yours may also be.

Trust the call and get support wherever you can. Free manuscript consults are available wherever there is a Writer-in-Residence. Seek them out. I did, and when Marie Clements said she found my work to be "dark and delicate," I was encouraged. Not only that, she introduced me to my publisher, Talonbooks, and a few years later, they published my first collection of poetry, *page as bone — ink as blood*. Don't be afraid to ask workshop providers and festival organizers if they have any subsidies, and if they don't, try to barter with them. Perhaps there is something you can do for them. Festival volunteers often get free passes to events. I have done this with my mentor, Betsy Warland. Some may not be able to offer this, as they don't need any assistance and need the income, but don't let that discourage you. Keep trying.

For those of you without a room of your own, there are coffee shops and libraries with Wi-Fi access if you need it. If you are like me, you might need uninterrupted quiet; even noise cancelling headphones are not enough. I need to be alone. One author, Gurjinder Basran, wrote an award-winning book, *Everything Was Goodbye*, as a mother working full-time. She created space for herself by getting up hours before her family. I live in a small one-bedroom apartment with my husband, and he simply goes to the park to play his sax when I need quiet time dedicated to writing. There may be options you have not yet explored. Look for them.

One of the most precious gifts you can give yourself is a routine. By this, I do not necessarily mean writing daily. Although many recommend this, I have never felt it was the right advice for me. Having said that, I do have rituals that I use to help me enter the creative space in my mind. I think of my writing life as a sacred calling and know that there is medicine in words, which have the power to heal or harm. At first, I thought this meant I needed to become the Indigenous Rumi, but what kept coming was stories of abuse. When I tried to write more "spiritual" stuff, it was limp-lipped dribbles of coded words I later learned to avoid. It took me nowhere. At first, I resisted writing, "yet again," about what my father and other men had done to me, until I learned to lean into what was coming. Some medicine tastes bad but does good. What if my story was not pleasant or spiritual? What if the magic lay in the truth-telling, in being fearless, in being that "dangerous old woman" that Clarissa Pinkola Estés speaks of? I am, after all, a member of what she calls the "Scar Clan." Resisting what wants to come through me is not wise, especially if I want to court grace.

None of this may be new to you. You may already know all this, but in my experience, when life gets busy, I can forget what I know. Protect yourself from busyness. Keep some empty spaces for contemplation, for taking walks or sitting on park benches. Whatever works for you. It may change over time, so watch for this. Learn to listen to what is being asked of you.

If I want to listen, I need to find and maintain a "room of my own" within my being. I light candles, and call and thank the ancestors when it is time to write. I make time for silence, for prayer, to smudge and lay tobacco. I attend to my sorrow and take long walks in the forest. It is there that I find grace.

What I mean by "grace," is that I enter a flow that brings me what I need. Just the other day, I was in the middle of editing an essay on language. The editor had pointed out the holes in my story, and I was struggling with how to fill in some missing information — information that I did not have access to. That week, my friend and Poet Elder, Joanne Arnott, sent me a book about some of the First Nations and Métis Elders from Portage la Prairie, a place we share a connection to. Within the book was an interview with my dad's cousin, and it contained the missing piece. That is grace in action.

You can do much to support grace happening more than it already does. Develop your own rituals. Spend time alone. Ask for assistance from the unseen world. How you do this will be guided by whatever teachings you follow. For some, it may simply be the muse. For others, it is God, Goddess, Creator, Allah, or your Ancestors. Even if you reject the notion of such things, what if your thoughts or prayers are sending signals to the collective unconscious, and someone will answer, just as Joanne Arnott did in my moment of desperation about that essay.

Our writing, or any creative endeavour, asks us to be responsive. Rigidity may backfire. We need to learn to listen for the nudges and cues, which are often subtle yearnings felt in the body. It may be something unexpected. You might feel pulled to watch a show in the middle of the afternoon, but you have a schedule. You promised yourself you'd sit and write for the whole afternoon. If you allow yourself this indulgence, it may spark something or bring words, thoughts, ideas, or concepts that enrich whatever you are currently working on.

With grace, there is less self-effort required. It is efficient. Why not court it by developing rituals to cue your body, mind, and spirit that we are entering the writing world. Why not make room for grace by leaving some empty space wherever you can? The time lost will be regained as you lean into synchronicities and become a good listener and follower, of whatever it is that is trying to make its way to you.

PROMPT:

Describe your ideal "room of your own." It may be internal or external — perhaps both. If it is a place, tell us how it feels to be there. What items are in the room, and why are they there? Is it small or large? Some of us like a vaulted ceiling with lots of light and space for our spirit to soar. Others may write best in a cocoon or a dark cave. Feel into what kind of internal and external atmosphere you need to do your best writing. What is it that your writing self longs for?

AUTOBIOGRAPHY OF THIS ESSAY

K. HO

1. I have a fear of the blank page. I struggle to put words down. It's not writer's block; I identify too pathologically with the faction of writers who don't believe in it. Instead, what I fear is that flat, mocking expanse of white.

2. On writing, Mary Ruefle notes: "among my fears can be counted the deep-seated uneasiness [...] that I consecrated my life to an imbecility [...] what I *think* I mean — by 'imbecility' is *something* intrinsically unnecessary and superfluous and thereby unintentionally cruel."[1]

3. I like the wryness of Ruefle's tone. Let me shield the world from my drivel! I am attracted to her words "unnecessary" and "superfluous", though I am unsure how to reconcile them with my empty page.

4. Federico García Lorca writes, "the poet who embarks on the creation of a poem [...] begins with the aimless sensation of a hunter about to embark on a night hunt through the remotest of forests. Unaccountable dread stirs in his heart."[2]

5. I like this idea, a writer traipsing through a dark tangled forest, sloshing through creeks, stumbling over roots. Writing as a form of psychic geography — a terrain of language, memory, or feeling — across which a writer must traverse.

6. Still, my fear of the blank page. If writing is an exercise of psychic geography, I worry that every word I inscribe brings me at once closer to, and further from, the landscape I am attempting to conjure. Said another way, I am not afraid of stepping into the dark forest; I am afraid of not breaking through the trees. I am afraid I will never reach the waiting horizon.

7. What is the horizon? I think this is a question I will return to again and again.

8. When I am first approached to contribute to this anthology, I email the editors and say, "Sounds great! I think I'd write something about the barriers to writing as a queer person of colour."

9. As an afterthought, I add a parenthetical clause to the email: "Sounds great! I think I'd write something about the barriers to (and joys of) writing as a queer person of colour."

10. (Why is joy always an afterthought?)

11. After sending the email, I say to myself: Yes, that's *right*. That's exactly what I will do: write an essay about being a person of intersecting marginalized identities. The essay will be *outstanding*. It will be *defiant* and *subversive* and *powerful*. It will resist tokenisation, destabilize singularity, *TRANSCEND ALL* —

12. But I could not write the essay.

13. I did not know how to.

14. More accurately, I did not want to.

15. It was only months later, after noticing my chest constrict every time I opened my laptop, that I realized I had done unto myself that which white supremacy does unto racialized writers: I had tokenised myself. No one had coaxed me into the topic — writing about identity — nor placed any parameters on me. I had decided to tackle it simply because I thought I should.

16. To be clear, I do believe that grappling with one's marginalisation in relation to writing can be a useful and generative pursuit. I just didn't want to anymore.

17. But isn't it important to write about identity? Toni Morrison famously said, "If there is a book you wish to read, but it has not been written yet, then you must write it."[3]

18. And yet Morrison also said, "The function, the very serious function of racism is distraction. It keeps you from doing your work. It keeps you explaining, over and over again, your reason for being."[4]

19. Where does identity end, and where does the work begin?

20. Is that a false binary? Am I marching toward the clearing, or am I lost in the thicket?

21. On the creative life of women (and trans)[5] artists, Audre Lorde writes, "The fear of our desires keeps them suspect and indiscriminately powerful, for to suppress any truth is to give it strength beyond endurance. The fear that we cannot grow beyond whatever distortions we may find within ourselves keeps us docile and loyal and obedient, externally defined [...]"[6]

22. Isn't it fascinating to notice what we internalize as queer writers of colour? What we think we're worth? What we're here for?

23. I want to write about topics because I *want* to write about them, not because I believe I should.

24. I think this is why I am attracted to Ruefle's deployment of "unnecessary" and "superfluous": because I do not experience excess or whim. When I look at the literary world, I do not see an abundance of voice, so much as an enduring erasure. This is not to say these voices like mine do not exist, but that they have long been refused. To write against silence is to carry the burden of representation. I have been lonely in so many rooms that I now assume an inflated

sense of responsibility: I fear I will fail my communities if I do not write the shape of myself — of us — alive. I do not know how to separate pure creative instinct from the tokenization I have internalized. I am underpractised in following desire.

25. What to do in this predicament? Try to pull it apart, I suppose. Articulate the tautology: I can't write my way out of being a queer writer of colour because I can't stop writing into it.

26. Identify ambition: I want so much to resist the contradiction of being pinned to identity, while feeling called to speak to it.

27. List everything else I wanted to write about: process, style, voice, rhythm, play, constraint, lyric, affect, atmosphere, genre, performance.

28. Lean on Ocean Vuong: "The line between desire and elimination, to me, can be so small. But that is who we are. There must be some beauty — and if not beauty, meaning — in that brutal power. I am still trying, and mostly failing, to find it."[7]

29. The truth of this essay is that I set out to destabilize the double-bind of being a queer writer of colour and instead found myself looping inside it. I wanted to write my way out of a problem and arrive somewhere new, but like Vuong, I think I am mostly failing — and perhaps for the better.

30. Perhaps this dialectic is for the better because failure is the point of writing. Writing, it seems to me, is about failure — is *of* failure. It asks us to inhabit the tension between what we want to conjure and what we ultimately put down. It asks to surrender to the alive, contradictory space between aspiration and attempt, success and defeat, and to keep trying anyway. Perhaps writing is less about breaking through the trees and reaching that elusive horizon, and more about coaxing the sentences to bend toward it, to arc.

31. If that is the case, I hope to tread the landscape carefully. I hope to walk slowly, to pause and observe the density of light filtering through the canopy. And I hope, above all, to glimpse in the distance, a different literary world — a rising city, a town square, a table, a garden, a road, a vista — and reach for it.

32. To reach, perhaps, it is time to start at the page.

1. Mary Ruefle, *Madness, Rack, and Honey* (Seattle: Wave Books, 2012), 103.

2. Quoted in Ruefle, *Madness,* 110.

3. Toni Morrison, Speech, Ohio Arts Council, Columbus, OH, 1981.

4. Toni Morrison, Keynote address, Portland State University, Portland, OR, 1975.

5. For a deeper discussion on language and trans inclusivity in Audre Lorde's work, see page 34 in adrienne maree brown's *Pleasure Activism.*

6. Lorde, Audre. (1984). Uses of the Erotic: The Erotic as Power. In *Sister Outsider: Essays & Speeches by Audre Lorde* (pp. 53-59). Crossing Press.

7. Spencer Quong, "Survival as a Creative Force: An Interview with Ocean Vuong," *The Paris Review,* June 5 2019.

PROMPT:

What do you want of your writing that you do not yet know you want? How do you want your writing to exist in the world, as a body of desire itself?

MINING FOR DETAILS: THE MOTHERLODE OF NON-FICTION

CLAUDIA CORNWALL

When you write non-fiction, you can't invent illuminating details that pull your readers in. You have to *find* those nuggets that engage your audience. My research typically starts with interviews, in which I plumb people's memories. But I often go further and weave in material from a variety of sources. First, I'll follow a traditional method, where I combine information gleaned from interviews and conversations with written and other archival materials; then, I'll look at how I can use social media to plunge my reader right into the middle of a fast-moving story.

For my first book, *Letter from Vienna: a daughter uncovers her family's Jewish past*, I visited libraries and archives. I studied yellowed newspaper clippings and read old letters written on fragile onion skin paper. I looked at diaries. I pored over maps and photographs. And I visited some of the places that figured in the book.

This memoir recounts what happened to my parents and grandparents in Germany and Austria during the 1930s and 1940s. My mother's father, Willi Frensdorff, was an engineer who worked for a shipyard in Bremen, AG Weser. Born to a Jewish family, he converted to Lutheranism when he married my grandmother. Despite that, life grew more and more difficult for him under the Nazis.

My mother told me that the director of Willi's shipyard, Franz Stapelfeldt, was aware of Willi's background, but supported him regardless. To ferret out the details of what he had done, I wrote to the city archive in Bremen. I received copies of newspapers, a booklet describing the history of Bremen during the Nazi period, and several pages of letters and memos that concerned an employee who was fired from the AG Weser shipyard in 1937.

The employee was Philipp Bechtloff, who had been informing high-ranking Nazi officials that AG Weser was employing Jews. Stapelfeldt found out about Bechtloff's activities, and on February 1, 1937, called him into his office. He said: "You know that Frensdorff is a Jew. You complained about him to the party, and you want to deprive him of his bread. You know that these days a Jew won't get a position anymore, and you know that Frensdorff is a patriot." The next day, Stapelfeldt did something surprising. He fired Bechtloff for what he termed were "security reasons." Now I knew about a specific measure Stapelfeldt had taken to defend my grandfather.

Another memo describes a chance encounter between Bechtloff and a shipyard employee called Mr. Gregor. Reading it, I could feel Bechtloff's fervid anger rippling off the page. On February 15, 1937, he was walking on Obernstraße (Obern street), past a transit stop for the No. 3 tram. When he spotted Gregor on his way to work, Bechtloff became highly excited and yelled, "It's all the fault of Mr. Stapelfeldt, Mr. Frensdorff, Mr. Kalweit, Mr. Behrens, and Miss Luer that I was fired. I'm going to denounce them in *Der Stürmer* and *Schwarzen Corps*. I will see to it that they lose their positions."

Despite Bechtloff's efforts, none of these people were fired. My grandfather was able to work at the shipyard until November 10, 1938 — Kristallnacht, the infamous night of broken glass. Then Willi was arrested, along with thirty thousand other Jewish men in Germany and Austria.

My mother couldn't remember where Willi was taken, but I understood from the booklet the city archive sent me, that many Jewish men arrested in Bremen on Kristallnacht were sent to Sachsenhausen, a concentration camp north of Berlin. The camp was preserved as a historical site, and when I wrote to the archive there, I learned that

Willi *was* a prisoner there, received a number, 10452, and was released on December 4. My mother had also told me that when Willi got home, he could no longer work, but Stapelfeldt paid him anyway. And that I was able to confirm. I found an entry in Willi's diary dated January 9, 1939: "Messenger brought salary." Six months later, Willi left Germany and escaped to Shanghai, the only place that would have him.

About a year after receiving documents from the city archive, I visited Bremen. I looked at a map and discovered that the No. 3 streetcars still ran out to the Weser River, as they had in my grandfather's day when the shipyard was there, at the end of the line. I saw that Obernstraße had only one stop where you could catch the No. 3 — in an older part of city, opposite the Karstadt department store. This was where Bechtloff had shouted at Gregor. When I went to the stop to have a look around, I could see the spires of the St. Petri Dom not far away. I snapped a picture, and a woman smiled at me approvingly. Then a No. 3 tram halted to pick up passengers. For a fleeting moment, I half expected the scene I had read about to play out before my eyes. The past was infiltrating my present, creating a state of mind in which it was easy to conjure up those events decades old.

Since I wrote *Letter from Vienna*, many archives have digitized their collections, making it much easier for writers to conduct research from the comfort of their own desks. A few clicks can retrieve documents and reports of many kinds. Digital photos are helpful, as are posts on Facebook and other social media platforms. They are not curated the way an archival collection is, but I realized their potential when I was writing my most recent book, *British Columbia in Flames: Stories from a Blazing Summer*. Because digital photos are timestamped, I was able to pinpoint an important and lucky shift of wind to precisely 9:35 p.m. on September 2, 2017. At 9:35 p.m., Facebook posts (also timestamped) helped me to establish the sequence of other events.

After a fire broke out at 100 Mile House on July 6, 2017, Lana Shields, who lives in Williams Lake, immediately began thinking about the horses that might be in danger. She wanted to be sure that they would have a safe place to stay and asked the directors of the Williams Lake Stampede Association whether she could shelter horses on the stampede grounds. They enthusiastically supported the idea. I know exactly when Lana set her initiative in motion from her Facebook post: "July 6, 7:20 p.m. Anyone needing a place for their horses due to the 100 Mile fire, please call me."

On July 7, a lightning storm ignited hundreds of fires all over the Cariboo and Chilcotin, and Lana told me that she knew, "This is gonna be a lot more than what we can probably handle." In the afternoon, at 3:13, she posted a message that she marked, "Urgent, Please Share." Lana explained that some people needed help transporting their horses to the grounds. Furthermore, she noted that she would require hay, water tubs, and buckets to look after the animals properly. Her message netted twenty-four comments and 273 shares. She was well on her way with her rescue mission. Later that afternoon, at 4:28, Lana appealed for someone with a class 1 license who could drive a stock trailer for people on Fox Mountain and the community of Wildwood. Ten minutes later, she put out a call for volunteers to help at the stampede grounds. Half an hour after that, she reported that Chris on Fox Mountain was asking for assistance with two horses and other critters. At 5:56 p.m., she forwarded an offer from Kristen who could haul two horses. At 6:24 p.m., Lana said she had more trailers on standby. "Call my cell," she posted, "I can't answer messages fast enough." At 7:29 p.m., she asked for more volunteers. At 7:54 p.m., she wrote that someone called Janice needed a ride for one horse. Finally, at midnight, Lana went to bed.

Lana and her team of volunteers ultimately rescued over three hundred horses over a period of four days. When she realized that Williams Lake itself was no longer safe, she began sending horses to a friend in Prince George who could accommodate them at an equestrian centre.

I documented the whole story, blow by blow. I felt like I was watching history unfold right in front of me. Thanks to Facebook — and also, of course, to Lana, who consented to my using her feed this way — I could convey how frantic the pace was and how much pressure Lana was under.

Whether relying on traditional sources or something more twenty-first century, digging into the details has surprised me and given me the means to engage readers and create an indelible impression, which is what we, as writers, are always striving to do.

PROMPT:

Tell a story using your favourite form of social media, Facebook, Twitter, etc. Or use your favourite form of social media as source material, and tell a story based on what you have learned.

BURSTING INTO IMAGERY: THE DANGEROUS POETIC PRESENT

PAUL HEADRICK

Writers often get asked if their work is autobiographical. Nobody asked me that about my novel *That Tune Clutches My Heart*, however, probably because the narrator, May, is a sixteen-year-old girl entering high school in 1948 — not much room for an autobiographical reading. But I did steal from my life for at least one bit. Early in the novel, one of May's classmates asks her an awkward question. She writes about the moment in her diary:

He spoke too loudly, and when several students sitting nearby laughed he went beet red. Let me correct that, for "beet" is hardly an original, vivid kind of red. He turned red, bright red, red as, well in fact he did not turn red at all, and if I cannot be imaginative with my simile I should be accurate. He turned pink.

That's about it for May's use of figurative language, and her reticence is a straight rip-off of my own. I'm cautious when it comes to similes and metaphors. It's the risk of a certain first person point of view that gets me: the "poetic present." I fear it.

Before I elaborate on the poetic present, consider two sentences, both including superbly effective similes:

They had a small, loud-playing band, and as we moved through the trees, I could hear the notes of the horns bursting like bright metallic bubbles against the sky.

It seemed as if life had been going on around me without my knowing it, in the disconcerting way that it sometimes does, like the traffic swirling past when one is standing on an island in the middle of the road.

The first example is from Ralph Ellison's short story masterpiece, "A Coupla Scalped Indians." (The title refers to a joke that the adolescent African American narrator makes at his own expense.) The simile conveys the joyous quality of the music, and it also dramatizes key features of the narrator's character: his youth, and his talent for imaginatively linking things we typically think don't go together — in this case, the aural and the visual. A few more images — there are only a few — with a similar structure confirm that this character-revealing feature of the simile isn't random. The narrator's consistent manner of expression embeds the story's compelling take on race and culture deep in his language.

The narrator of the second example, from Barbara Pym's subtle comic novel *A Glass of Blessings,* is in her thirties, with a more pedestrian sensibility than Ellison's protagonist. Near the end of the novel, she begins to see how her conventionality has blinded her to the potential of the lives around her. She's a Londoner, and it makes sense that the image of someone standing on an island with dense traffic whizzing past occurs to her as she reflects on her recent past. Her simile is vivid, but not as striking as the synesthesia of Ellison's young narrator, so it's consistent with her way of thinking. She's intelligent but unimaginative, and her limitation is important in the novel. Pym never succumbs to the temptation to drop a more striking image that might superficially impress while violating the consistency of the character, even at this moment, when the narrator is having something of an epiphany.

In short, both similes show the authors to be in fine control over figurative language and what it reveals about their narrators.

Here are two more examples. Something could be said for each, but I think there's a grave literary problem here:

I moved to a window seat and watched through the bright mists the fields form-
ing their regiments, in full parade order, the sad shires, like an army the size
of England. Then the city itself, London, as taut and meticulous as a cobweb.

With my free hand, I moved to take Ai-ming's coat, remembering too late she
didn't have one. My arm wavered in the air like a question mark.

The first example is from Martin Amis's *London Fields.* The comparison
of the fields to regiments is vivid, and we can imagine the narrator
making it at the moment of his approach to London, but it's not clear
what "in full parade order" adds to the picture or how the fields would
suggest the hierarchy of such an order. The phrase "the sad shires," an
allusion to Wilfred Owen's World War I poem "Anthem for Doomed
Youth," though it has a military connotation that's consistent with the
metaphor, just seems like an interruption. It suggests that the narrator
isn't thinking of the fields as regiments at all — they're not regiments
if they're shires. The second sentence shows the narrator abruptly no
longer thinking in military terms — and it's puzzling. In what sense
could sprawling, swirling London appear from the air to be "meticulous" or "taut"? The narrator is a writer, and his flamboyant voice draws
attention to him instead of what's being described, suggesting his self-
admiration. But the narrator's egotism feels like an excuse for authorial
self-indulgence rather than an integral feature of the narrative.

In the second example, from Madeleine Thien's *Do Not Say We*
Have Nothing, the narrator is a girl of ten, though the perspective
sometimes shifts to that of her adult self. At a moment of emotional
intensity, she's conscious of the gesture she makes. The perspective is
the girl's; it would be a strain to imagine the adult recalling a spontaneous movement she made some decades earlier. Even if the line
expresses the girl's point of view, however, it's awkward. What child
has such an awareness of gestures as she makes them? Perhaps she is
preternaturally aware of her body and its movements — novels aren't
obligated to give us narrators whose ways of thinking are typical —
but that possibility isn't developed by further images.

Another striking feature of these novels: similes and metaphors proliferate in them, and it's very difficult to make them cohere with the character of the narrator, in contrast with the way Ellison's and Pym's images cohere. That proliferation is a key element of their point of view: the poetic present. In the poetic present, there's an awful lot of figurative language, and it doesn't consistently, specifically, reveal character. The narrator looks back on the past from a present "poetic" moment, in which experience is filtered through a special sensibility. That sensibility translates the immediate responses and observations of the earlier time into more subtle, evocative, or just attention-getting figurative expressions of the same sensations. The only connection between language and character is a very general one: the translation endows that earlier self with sensitivity and beauty, even if, or particularly if, those early sensations involve pain. Or, as in the case of Amis's novel, what's communicated is the narrator's flamboyance, and the language is distancing because, instead of caring about the character, we're only moved to say "wow."

Amis is a literary giant. Thien's *Do Not Say We Have Nothing* won the Scotiabank Giller Prize, the Governor General's Award, and was shortlisted for the Man Booker Prize. I've chosen examples from these two highly acclaimed writers in order to show how even the best can succumb to it, can be tempted — perhaps by a facility for striking imagery, or maybe a belief that such imagery is what raises storytelling to capital "L" Literature, to art.

It must be that readers who enjoy the poetic present don't expect consistency between character and expression. They don't ask what figurative language reveals about the narrator, accepting this unusual feature of the narrator's voice as a convention. Perhaps it's something like the convention of the Broadway musical, in which characters burst into song at moments of heightened emotion. We don't watch a musical and demand to know why the characters are always singing. That's how it works. In novels written in the poetic present, the narrator regularly bursts into imagery. For those who enjoy fiction of this kind, it must be that that's how the poetic present works, though it conflicts with another, older novelistic convention, that of psychological realism.

For many readers, the convention works well. I know that I'm in a minority when I resist the poetic present, but I also know that I'm not alone, and resist I do. I want to quarrel with the authors. This simile here, why does the narrator say this? Why would this metaphor occur to the narrator at such a moment, or at any time? Wait, that's five attention-getting similes in five pages — what are you trying to show about your narrator?

Reviewers often describe such fiction as poetic, or lyrical, or transcendent. When I read such comments in jacket blurbs, I'm almost certain of what I'll discover in the novels themselves, and that I'll find it false. The implausibility of the poetic present and the distracting language its narrators use adds up to the strange impression that the authors lack a kind of belief in their narrators and their worlds. If they did believe, they wouldn't have their narrators speak that way, a way that contradicts other things we know about them or is inconsistent with the world the fiction creates. Finally, if the authors don't believe, how can we?

I said that in my own novel, the simile that the narrator doesn't complete is about the only instance of figurative language in the whole work. She does, however, make one more attempt in the final line:

It was dark by the time we returned, and as we drove by Maple Grove Park we passed through a flurry of spring moths that turned golden in our headlights, like flecks of magic dust scattered by the Good Witch of the North.

Surely no reader has ever reached that sentence and thought, "Aha! A simile! The narrator has, at last, overcome her anxious perfectionism and grown up!" So, in signaling the protagonist's coming-of-age, in small part, by finally allowing her a fanciful image, I was indulging myself. Even if nobody was going to notice, I wanted the narrator, at the moment when she takes a step forward, to feel a freedom to be youthful in her description and to take some pleasure in the persistence of her innocence.

Did I succumb? With that one simile, did I violate something I'd established in May's character? Reading the line now, I can find myself regretting my self-indulgence. In any case, readers will decide. But I imagine May growing up to be a writer, one more adventurous than I with her similes and metaphors, but also careful, attentive to what words reveal, untempted by the poetic present.

PROMPT:

Write a short paragraph, in the first person, in which the narrator describes being engaged in a solitary, physical activity. It can be any activity: washing dishes, climbing a mountain. Make no reference to the narrator's feelings or thoughts. Use no figurative language.

Read the paragraph over, and make notes about what the actions and the words describing them reveal about the narrator.

Imagine the paragraph as the beginning of a short story. Make notes about how events in the story might challenge the narrator in relation to those personal qualities the paragraph reveals.

THE POWER OF ADJACENCY

ROB TAYLOR

Think back to your favourite moments in your reading life. Not your favourite books, per se, but your favourite scenes or sentences or lines: the moments that made you fall in love with writing or pulled you into a deeper relationship with the word; the moments that spurred you on the path that led you to pick up this book; the moments that, if you're lucky, you'll one day be able to create for others. If you're honest, do you think of those moments as belonging exclusively to their author? Or are they also, in some way, yours?

I think of some of my favourites — Gollum's riddles in the dark, Frost's puzzled horse, Williams's wheelbarrow and chickens (no, Williams's red and white), Rukeyser's islands, Carver's cathedral, Cavafy's Ithaca, Issa's dry creek and lightning — and they are truly *mine*. You've probably read at least some of those stories and poems, but you didn't read the same things I did. Not because your capacity to understand what's on the page is any different from mine, but because you'll never be able to "read" all I've added to these moments (just as I won't for you): imagined backstory, subtext, argument, idiosyncrasies of voice, image ... all the connective tissue I've strung together as my contribution to a co-authorship that's fully accessible to no one but myself, not even the author.

It's co-authorship that turns a moment in literature eternal (or, at least, life-long for that particular reader). But how do we, as writers, encourage such engagement from our readers? How do we produce something that sticks to them so tightly that it becomes part of their larger life, its logic and arguments somehow their own? I believe we do this by enacting our thought patterns on the page, so the words can more readily facilitate the merger of our minds with those of our readers. We leap from image to image, scene to scene, in unexpected ways. We link associatively. We create gaps between what happened last and what happens next and leave it to our readers to fill them in.

But that's not how I think, you say? Close your eyes right now and start counting sheep, as if invoking sleep. How long do you last before your mind wanders, and in what wild direction does it go (perhaps the place it arrives at is mundane, but remember, that a moment ago, you were in a farmer's field)? Try this again before you sleep tonight, and the effect will be doubled, the near-dormant mind doing its pre-slumber calisthenics, readying for the dream state.

It's easy, especially when in a workshop setting with other writers, to succumb to the cult of clarity. Everyone has their questions about a piece of writing: *What am I supposed to see? What does that mean? Was anyone else really lost here?* Working towards greater clarity in your writing is important, especially when it comes to precision of meaning: you should know what you're trying to say and do your best to say it. But if we race around amending our writing to answer each and every question a reader might pose, we leave no room for that reader's co-authorship. The writing becomes flat, utilitarian — easy to consume and easy to forget. And it truncates what you really want to say, which is elusive and expansive, and which exists above and beyond what you are *actively* attempting. In pursuing greater clarity, we create mental worlds which in no way resemble our own.

Our lives are chaotic, filled with random data we organize into narratives. More of our lives are spent constructing, maintaining, questioning, and transforming those narratives than are spent "living" them. In fact, we never really "live" them in a pure sense. Our brains make and make and make the lives we think of as unfurling effortlessly before us. Our brains are rarely more "alive" than when they get to create in new ways, using materials they've never before brought together, materials provided by some other mind and transmitted to them in writing. This isn't to say that a work of prose or poetry should show the world as we live it in its entirety — of course not, fitting all of the chaotic random data of the world into a story or essay or poem would be impossible. We will always have to focus and streamline significantly in order to tell our particular story. But it is to say that the lasting moments in that story, the ones that feel authentic and owned by the reader, are the moments that mirror our real-life engagement with the world. They are the moments where the reader is given the space to make their own connections between disparate items; to wonder and assemble.

I like to call this central gift of the writer — the ability to pock the linear with collaborative gaps — the "power of adjacency." We put one disparate thing beside another and leave the rest to the reader. "The power of adjacency" can manifest as metaphor or simile (two images/ideas placed close together), as word play or rhyme (two words placed close together), as metre (two syllables placed close together), as tension (two characters placed close together), etc., etc., etc. Adjacency sits at the very heart of literature, language, and our waking and sleeping thought.

Writing in *Scientific American*, Earnest Hartmann theorized that dreaming helps us connect up or weave our recent lived experiences in with our stored memories of similar events. Researchers have found that people who survive trauma are more likely to have traumatic dreams following the incident — not of the trauma itself but of something adjacent to it (someone who escaped a burning building may dream of being swept from a beach by a tidal wave, for instance). This provides them a way to process the emotion of the event abstractly. Hartmann writes:

Thus we consider a possible [...] function of a dream to be weaving new material into the memory system in a way that both reduces emotional arousal and is adaptive in helping us cope with further trauma or stressful events. (Scientific American, *July 14, 2003*)

I suggest the best, most lasting stories, essays, and poems mirror this process and hopefully to a similar effect. They present the opportunity for surprising, and perhaps difficult, connections and invite the reader to, within the safety of literature, puzzle their way across the gaps. And they make us more resilient to future upheavals.

This process, of course, comes with great risk. Not every reader will cross the gap with you, and even fewer will feel altered by the process. To enter deep into someone's mind and heart is not easy. As humans, we are varied and come to great writing at varied times. Often, we are not the right person, or we are not yet ready. Even the greatest works of literature only change some of the people, some of the time. The question for you, as a writer, is: *Do I want to try?* Transparent writing has its place, and that place pays better. You have to ask yourself if that's worth jettisoning a chance at transformative connection.

In *Why Poetry* (Ecco, 2017), Matthew Zapruder describes poetry as "a constructed conversation on the frontier of dreaming." I would say this same phrase could describe all literary language, and, perhaps, I would modify the end to say: "the frontier of waking and sleeping thought." It's a verisimilitude that we writers and readers are always pursuing, with the hope that, at some unpredictable moment, two adjacent minds might reach across the page and become one.

PROMPT:

How do we refresh our similes and metaphors? How do we inject little gaps — fresh opportunities for associative connections — into our writing? Here's a fun exercise, originally taught to me by the poet Kate Braid, which can shake up your head and help you create more playful and surprising associations in your writing:

1. Think about two activities you do regularly enough, both of which have specialized terminology associated with them. Choose activities that are important to you (though they do not have to be things you *like*). Now, take five to ten minutes to write, in two

separate lists, as many specialized words as possible that you associate with each activity. (For instance, if you play tennis, associated words would be "racket," "serve," "court," "baseline," etc.) Try to get down every last thing you can think of for each of the two activities.

2. Read over the two lists of words. Select the one whose words you're most drawn to, and label it "List A." Label the other one "List B."

3. Take ten minutes to freewrite (don't stop to edit what you've written or think through what you might write next) about conducting the "List B" activity but using the vocabulary from "List A." An example: if your "List A" was "Writing" and "List B" was "Running," you might start "Page after page, his footfalls ink the dusty trail..." Your mission (if you choose to accept it!) is to integrate every term on your "List A" into your "List B"-themed freewrite before the time runs out.

4. If you write something brilliant, wonderful! If not, look for lines or phrases here or there that might be useful elsewhere in your writing. And, more generally, allow the process to loosen your mind a bit; let associations gather more freely, one idea filtering through another, and go where those associations take you.

A MOMENT FOR THE CRAFT: POETRY

JOANNE ARNOTT

In the years I devoted to the thinking of essence and representation, I thought a poem must be new, original, "only new," wei xin 唯新*, that is, ri ri xin, you ri xin* 日日新, 又日新, *"make it new, daily new." But after I got the concept of reincarnation, I felt that sometimes traditional elements or reflections appeared in my poems, which in my earlier days I could not accept, or would even be scared of, but I accept them with ease now [...] Now I regard the history of literature and painting as a process of unceasing reincarnation, which leaves behind many traces.[1]* — Che Qianzi

Poetry is a most ancient form of literature, rising up all over the world. It exists at the intersection of oral traditions and textual traditions. Every tradition has its own rules that morph and change over time. If we imagine all possible genres as people standing shoulder to shoulder, poetry may be found standing between prayer and song — or between calligraphy and carving.

Poetry and poetic or lyric prose are language sensitive systems, culturally sensitive systems. Influences and cross–fertilizations between literatures and languages is ongoing. Translations are the lifeblood of poetry, developing interface between language groups and aesthetics. A few examples of broadly influential, much-translated texts (one, many, or divine authorship): *The Vedas, Tripiṭaka, Daodejing, Talmud, Koran, The Bible* ... The classics, the canon, the poetry shared colloquially and taught in schools, emanate and innovate from these diverse, ancient centres, both oral and textual.

What we love, what we consider excellence, what we consider worth noting, is flexible and open to influence. Oral and literary text traditions flow through us — we are points of confluence, places of congruence — we are the world making sense of itself.

Writing is a negotiation with reality, not the creation of one. There's knowledge that exists in our cultures, in our languages that's the result of other earlier encounters with the real. We can benefit from it by knowing what words have become or are coming to mean about the world.[2] — Daniel David Moses

Oral influences: what did I hear?
Text traditions: what did I read?

Exercise:
Take a moment to consider your whole life from this perspective: in my early life, what were my oral influences? What were my textual influences? How have these changed over time? How are each of these reflected in my current work?

We also tend to express our local geographies, both where we are now and where we have been over the years, drawing upon the lineages and traditions that are most relevant in the moment for form and style and content. In the simplest sense, our bodies are the local geography through which all other realms are experienced, each with our unique weathers and climates within.

Breath is a governing value; we use our breath to measure our words, to express our inspirations. The diversity of poetic forms, from strict rhyme schemes to traditional aesthetic associations, are linked to the breath and to the sound, feeling, and memory of language spoken.

Poetry exists as both oral and text expressions: we decide how to place our words on the page in such a way that the reader will understand our meaning and have a sense of how to recreate our words aloud. My invitation to the reader is to explore embodiment and breath as bases for your own writing, editing, and performance.

this is a title

this is a poem, or
this may be just a few lines
set down in the place of a poem.
this is text. this is an expression of a textual nature.[3]

In working with writers at every stage of career, I encourage the use of freewriting.[4] It is both a way to clear the mind and a way to capture raw material — the dross of daily life. It can be used on your own or as a ritual of group practice. Basically, you set a time — five minutes, ten minutes — and you write, nonstop, for the duration. If you can't think of what to write, rely on your senses — what do you hear? What do you feel? What do you taste, smell? What do you see? Do not go back for anything: do not cross out, don't worry about spelling; all this can be sorted out later. You begin, and you keep spilling words until the time ends.

Exercise:
• *Freewrite for ten minutes.*
• *Identify the most compelling words and phrases.*
• *Strip these out of your original text and place them in a list on a fresh page.*
• *Consider different ways to sequence these words and phrases to create the most interesting and most melodious presentations.*
• *Write a few different possible poems, adding bridging words or concepts as needed, remain succinct.*

Once you have (by whatever means) raw text, begin by reading it aloud, listening for form and pattern within the words. At every stage of revision — writing, polishing, responding to critique — return to the oral; let the song behind the words be your guide.

Avoid abstraction, use sensual or sensory-based images to recreate your meaning (see sample poem below). Consider the reader in select-ing the sequence of images and where to break the line to emphasize or de-emphasize words and images.

Punctuation is wholly optional: you can recreate the short and long pauses of prose — the comma, semi-colon, colon, period, dash — through spacing of words on a line, line breaks, and verse stanza or verse paragraph spacing and placement. Full sentences are also wholly optional: we use the power of suggestion and the rhythms of our words to create *meaning*.

My approach is very direct. The principles are vitality (energy, life force, qi), beauty (patterns, parallels, disruptions), and brevity (succinct, suggestive).

Through poetry, we may tell a story or paint a picture; we may point to the moon, provoke thought, inspire emotion or spiritual uplift — or downdrift — but we are not required to do any of these things. A puzzle, a joke, a memory, a cosmos: each poem has its preferences, and our job as a poet is to remove unnecessary weight and let the poem fly.

Poetry may be a form of divine play, but it is also as ordinary as breathing or brushing your hair. Creativity is a natural human function. As bodies, we absorb and hold the world, and we express and create the world. We are of the world, not separate. We are a form of nature. Poetry is one of many possible channels for us in our making.

a moment for the craft: beer

The colours of beer and the ways they do
or do not allow light to filter through —

standing quietly in a tall glass, a cup of window —
pale yellows to broody reds and ambers, to deepest browns —

The head, suggestive of oceanplay —
ranging in colour and texture, density and depth —

Whether or not
small realms or marbles of air
flick into being and rise —

small realms or drops of water
form into being and descend
in counterpoint —

The beauty of beer —
my fondness for it —
muscular medicine —

loosening agent for
the body fraught[5]

1. "Poetics as Reincarnation: A Conversation with Che Qianzi," Glenn Mott, *Chinese Literature Today* (2018)

2. "An Interview with Daniel David Moses," Joanne Arnott, *Contemporary Verse 2* (2007)

3. Joanne Arnott, *Pensive & beyond* (Nomados 2019)

4. Peter Elbow, *Writing Without Teachers*. New York: Oxford UP, 1973, 1-7.

5. Justyna Krol (TWS 2020) led a writing workshop for our group, the students suggested the topic: beer. This was my sensory-based response (sight, feeling).

HOW I LEARNED, AM LEARNING: AN ESSAY

GEORGE BOWERING

1.

Greater than his brother Joe,
Dominic DiMaggio
                    had signature
octagonal centre field wire framed
eyeglasses.

            I didn't have my specs
yet, but I agreed with the Fenway
song, knowing objectivity might
get you somewhere in baseball
business, but look, we Red Sox
swim in caramel-thick sentimentality.

                    People,
old and young, think they know
something, discount us for
writing poems about baseball.

Worse,
they call it a USAmerican
game, proving they have been too quick
in their reading of Jane Austen.

I don't
like her much, but I give them
Jane Austen, though I don't
give Barney and his Google brothers
a second step before I pick them off.

I mean I Googled when I might have
Gogoled, asked for
"his brother Joe"
and learned
how and why his brothers
didn't care for him.

Not because of some
overcoat, I'll admit, though
April nights can get cold
above the Red Sox bullpen.

2.

Thinking with my old bones
in bed of an early afternoon,

how seldom I am permitted
to return to a meadow,

nor even touch its image
          with the fingers of my mind,

a four-seam fastball
on the outside corner
of Robert Duncan's house.

It would have been nothing to him
had he learned that a baseball
fell into Robin Blaser's glove
in my dream this morning.

        They were not greater
than one another; they were brother
poets,
        and our purpose is to read them
(and write them) and not to engage in
ex-
planation.

3.

Baseball is too easy
        an allegory, poetry
is not,
        Mexico is not,
travel is not poetry,
        poetry

is the command to be still
    and see whether She

sends it to you,
something
like a fly ball that
catches *you.*

Bless you

standing alone on the perfect grass

all the ears of poetry
turned away
while you experience
what has not
yet happened.

Deep in their untroubled hearts
a few know what you are seeing,
a few
turn away serenely
from disdainful faces,

the saddest of possible words
an absolute necessity
for the listener
who would catch
what he knows is catchable,
and never glimpse it full,
never that close,
out there alone.

4.

When we were published tyros,
those professors and old anthologized poets

said we had to work long
            to become masters.

                        The first
intelligent thing we said back
            was that poetry
            didn't want masters,

those ginks who knew what was
            waiting at the end
            of the next line.

        They are rewarded,
                        such is their aim,
upon mastering the art of something,

            oh magister, oh dare we say it?

            Oh magistrate

proposing masterpieces
            masterworks
            master ———

oh magnify your accomplishment.

Ah, no.

Right now I'm waiting for *this* piece
to tell me where I went wrong.

I have a fair portion of my heart
left,
let it not impose
nor expose

but turn to the words and ask those
what are we doing?

5.

Robert Duncan and Dom DiMaggio,
San Francisco heroes . . . .

It didn't do any good to
pretend you'd fallen asleep;
Duncan
would continue talking. It was the world
he spoke to,
the strike zone he pitched around.

He didn't even have a brother Joe,

The Little Perfessor never read his poems,
never sat on someone's kitchen chair
to watch an old fashioned

stage, as they say, production
with Attic overtones

while Robert never went to
Seals Stadium to watch
with one eye
a great play in the ninth
that had the spectators
trembling in the cold
till just then.

6.

I played ball in glasses,
sometimes breaking them,
sometimes reading our catcher's poems
as if they were signs
between innings.

Now I wear a baseball cap
frontward on my size 8 head.
I wear the Red Sox cap.
I wear the San Francisco cap.
I never wear
that most beautiful one, the cap worn by his
brother Joe.
The one worn by Japanese tourists
and would-be model girls.

If I'm in New York I wear the cap
once worn by the Visalia Oaks.

7.

And over the green fields wilted down under your blaze....
of all hidden things I sing,   waiting for evening's grace.

Casually, a woman invented by Jane Austen
told us Catherine was off
playing baseball, aged fourteen.

                        I smile when I
think of Jane sitting in a drawing room
with Jack Spicer.
                        She wouldn't have
liked his clothes, but she would have
shown us how they were interesting.

People, here and there,
        think they know better,
        suffer us for quoting Jane Austen
        about adolescent sport,

        but I'll bet I would have been half
        in love with Catherine Morland.

8.

I have powerful friends in Ottawa,
friends of Poetry, language of the gods.

You can look forward to poetry in your life,
leave obedient prose behind,
leave social anxiety behind.

After Washington sends warplanes
          to bomb small countries,
Ottawa must drop bilingual poems
          onto the ruins.

9.

Oh, that's not my subject.
My subject ———

here's how it began, apparently.
The female friend of a male friend
told him that speaking of me,
· however hoarsely, she demanded that she must have me.

I'm speaking of Jane Austen. Apparently
she spoke of me as her centre fielder.

Can you imagine? Henry, she called me
and sometimes Little Dom.

I was not greater than my brother.
My brother could do a hundred
things I could not do.

PROMPT:

When my dad was playing catch with me and teaching me how to catch the ball, the first and most important thing he told me was "receive the ball; don't fight it." Don't stab at it, take it as the matador says, "*recibiendo*." When he was teaching me basketball and it came to dribbling, he said let it come to you; don't smack it. Maybe such a principle occurs in other sports, but I've never spent much time watching or playing other sports.

But I sure recognize it in composing poetry. Letting the ground ball come to you and then applying your skill to it is a lot like what happens when you are in the middle of composing a poem. In the better parts of "How I Learned," stuff came to me, words and the equally important punctuation, including line-ends. I call this principle respect for the language, which (who) is older than I am, more experienced than I am, and more precise than I am. When they talk about a poet's "gift," this is unbeatable.

In baseball, as in poetry, you learn by reading and figuring out what previous players have done. Then you practice and practice. I would see how Bobby Doerr or Jack Robinson started a double play and try doing it a hundred times. (My models were gone, but I was still working at it in my early sixties.) Then I would ask myself why it seemed in my reading out loud of H.D. she seemed so *receiving* of the words and Robert Frost seemed like some old guy giving advice.

In his most famous poems, Frost begins by making a statement, and ends by making sure you get the moral of his story. One of his most quoted poems is "Mending Wall," which opens this way: "Something there is that does not love a wall." While we are thinking, yeah, yeah, it's Frost. We are also thinking what does he get by putting the first three words backward, except to sound sort of biblical. Then along comes the anecdote, in which the grand old Poet contrasts himself favourably to his neighbour who spouts clichés while helping to instill order in nature. A reader has to supply her own irony in remarking that the poet, with his regular blank verse, is doing likewise. The poet, as much as the neighbour, is using his mastery to keep his line straight. When Alexander Pope, a very witty poet, once wrote that true wit is nature to advantage dressed, he knew who was taking advantage.

Have a listen to "Oread," a short poem by H.D. She composed it in language you might expect of a supplication, perhaps the opposite of mastery.

Try a contrast between W.H. Auden and W.C. Williams. They both wrote famous poems about Pieter Brueghel's famous painting *Landscape with the Fall of Icarus*. Both poems, Auden's "Musée des Beaux Arts" and Williams' "Landscape with the Fall of Icarus," are in their ways about the unconcern surrounding the boy's enormous fall. Auden uses it as one of his examples of a point he is making at the beginning of the poem. As Frost would begin a poem with his topic sentence, and then launch an anecdote about not liking artificially measured human organizing of nature while he does just that to language, Auden also begins with the statement, "About suffering they were never wrong, The Old Masters," and then gives us examples of paintings in which suffering is ignored by nearby people.

Auden is good at hitting home with his argument and its conclusions. He wants us, I'll bet, to say that he was not wrong, that he is a later master, though he was thirty-eight when he composed the poem. As you know by now, that is not what I would call a good relationship between artist and the world or the work.

Now look at Williams's poem. It first appeared in his last book, published when the poet was seventy-nine years old. Like Auden's, his poem was in part the result of a visit to an art gallery. Williams wrote a series of poems in response to a collection of Brueghel paintings. He does not try to *use* the painting to make a point. The poem proceeds to say what was happening to the language in Williams's head while he was looking at the picture. Whereas Auden in his poem was teaching, Williams in his poem is learning. Thus it begins "According to Brueghel/ when Icarus fell/ it was spring" and ends "unsignificantly/ off the coast/ there was// a splash quite unnoticed/ this was/ Icarus drowning."

I notice a lot of things there. Here are three: one's eye and voice travel down the poem as someone's eye travelled down the painting; there is some lovely natural rime there; Williams says in fourteen lines what Master Auden took a whole page to say.

You know how? Dr. Williams situated himself before the art: *recibiendo.*

POETRY IN PROSE — CROSSING GENRES OR AND NOW A WORD FROM OUR SPONSORS

MADELINE SONIK

In my childhood home, our television played from the break of day to the station's midnight sign-off. An American flag, flapping in the wind to "The Star-Spangled Banner," would appear, or, on occasion, a U.S. military plane, soaring through the heavens, accompanied by John Gillespie Magee's sonnet "High Flight."

Needless to say, this was before streaming services and even cable, a time when fathers "slipped the surly bonds of earth" (as Magee famously penned) and climbed the perilous heights of suburban roofs to install primitive metal antennas that looked like racks of coat hangers and had the habit of "going on the fritz."

It's likely that I did hear Magee's poem, blaring from the living room, some sleepless midnights just before the lulling hum of television static filled my ears, but I imagine far more influential in my evolving life as a writer were the subliminal language lessons taught to me by commercials.

Commercials, after all, were numerous and repetitive and constructed, specifically, to catch the viewer's attention. There were jingles, I still recall, like the Rice Krispies' onomatopoeic *snap, crackle, pop* theme, and slogans containing similes: "Ajax Liquid cleans like a white tornado." I unconsciously absorbed the engaging rhythms and poetic techniques television commercials employed, and when I began writing, I have no doubt that that early barrage of advertising, something the parent-teacher association in our community denounced as harmful, had laid a foundation for my future literary forays.

Reviewers often comment that I bring my skills as a poet to my prose. In many cases, this happens organically, the result, not only of the bombardment of television advertising in childhood, but also the conscious efforts I've made throughout my life to dissect and absorb the inspired voices of other writers. Sometimes, however, when poetic spontaneity fails and the prose piece I'm working on demands a lyrical dimension, I'm forced to turn to my knowledge of specific time-honored devices and techniques — the kind you find in poetry, as well as in advertising.

Consider the following passage from my retold fairy tale "The Mermaid":

Beginning where the gravel road grew vague at the end of Monica Street, the field spread lake-like. It opened past the dying maples, the reedy swamp, the abandoned and twisted mufflers of the car graveyard, past a grey shack, out in waves of swelling stink grass, to the sooty oil-soaked spines of the railroad ties. Beyond this, a farmer had built his house, and just beyond that, the welling city of Fontainebleau merged with a highway that extended all the way to Toronto, with a line running through its back, straight and white as a skunk.

Perhaps the first thing that will strike you about this poetic passage is the concrete sensory detail. The reader is given particulars rather than abstractions: *lake-like fields*; *dying maples, reedy swamps*. Specificity can turn a vague object — *grounds, tree, wetlands* — into resonant images that say much more than generic nouns.

Metaphors are another device used both in versification and television commercials that summon the spirit of poetry into prose. For example, "waves of swelling stink grass" will make an ocean of the fetid fields beyond the grey shack. The reader will hold in her mind a tension of images that not only enlarge the story's canvas but also, due to their unlikely proximity, provide a stimulating point of engagement, a place in which the reader's literal sensibilities are forced to expand.

Notice, also in this example, the device of alliteration ("swelling stink") that continues, hissing snake-like: "to the sooty oil-soaked spines of the railroad ties." Further, notice that these inanimate "ties" have been transformed by "spines" into creatures with the poetic device of personification, as has the highway, "with a line running through its back." Additionally, there's a simile at the end of the passage to enhance the personification and compare this throughfare's markings to those of a skunk.

Indeed, there are few such devices that show up in poems and commercials that can't, in some way, be strong-armed into the service of prose. The trick, however, is to make sure that the ones you select are appropriate for the task at hand and don't jar or overwhelm the narrative flow. Other common devices that I've found easily transplant to prose, though not exemplified in the passage above, include repetition, hyperbole, and onomatopoeia.

One tool I frequently use, widespread in poetry and television ads, is "the listing technique." As a tot, I must have taken in that Bosco syrup was "extra rich, extra thick, extra chocolatey," that Old Gold cigarettes were "the smoothest, mildest, tastiest, cigarette ever created," and that Sugar Smacks, according to Clark Kent, were "puffs of wheat, sugar toasted, and candy sweet."

Before I was ever cognisant of poetry's similarities to "words from our sponsor," my mind had ingested many of the literary devices used on Madison Avenue. The use of lists in poetry remained unknown to me until I entered university, as did the catalogue poem, a type that relies upon lists for its construction. In this form, words are carefully selected and work to a specific purpose, often creating the effect of a chant or a prayer. But even poetry of more diverse forms may be composed of lists. For example, Elizabeth Barrett Browning's well-known sonnet that begins "How do I love thee? Let me count the ways" continues with a quantitative inventory of the proportions of her love. By listing in this way, intangible emotion is transformed into something measurable and concrete.

"The listing technique" can be called upon to create a wide range of diverse effects in prose. In the example I provide above, see how the list, which encompasses the entire passage, has been composed to convey movement. The reader follows the outstretching geography of the mythical city of Fontainebleau past field, tree, and swamp, past junkyard, shack, and railroad tracks, past a farmhouse right out to the highway and beyond. I was attempting to create the sensation one might experience in a low-flying helicopter or as a disembodied spirit surveying the land. The land is important in this story, as it is in the entire collection, and so poetically framing it, as I do in the passage above and in other passages throughout the collection, is not out of keeping with the logic of the narrative.

Notice also how the listing technique, as used here, imposes a relentless kind of rhythm. Just as in poetry and television advertising, rhythm is an important element in prose. If I'd wished to make the rhythm less relentless, I could have inserted conjunctions or broken the list up into several sentences. I was hoping, however, to increase the pace of the story and, in so doing, produce the blood-pumping anxiety that underscores the work.

One final note to keep in mind when infusing prose with poetic devices is the importance of language. Be aware that every word contains a rhythm, a meaning, and an emotional resonance. As you place word beside word, you produce melody as well as text (or in the world of commercials, jingles as well as slogans). Not only will a thesaurus be your friend in this pursuit, but any relevant reference material that offers the precise language of accurate detail will be helpful.

PROMPT:

Write a short poetic prose piece predominantly of lists. If you wish to write non-fiction, try:

    a) a childhood birthday party,

    b) your most profound memory, or

    c) why you like to visit a particular city.

For fiction,

    a) a haunting,

    b) a secret, or

    c) a treasure.

Before you begin this exercise, research your topic to discover specific details and language that might be useful and inspirational.

In writing the piece, use as many of the following poetic devices as possible, keeping in mind that you want them to enhance, rather than flood, the narrative: metaphor, simile, repetition, alliteration, onomatopoeia, and personification.

THE PERFECT SETTING: EVERYWHERE AND NOWHERE

JOAN B. FLOOD

When I decided to write *Left Unsaid* — a story about people wanting to do the right thing according to their beliefs and conscience, and the result leaving them to wonder if less pain and tragedy would have happened if they hadn't — I knew I wanted to explore the characters and subject far from the modern world of internet, Facebook, cell phones, and other social media. It's hard to explain exactly, but I wanted to explore something very private to these characters, something out of the reach of the "no sooner done than said" of our technological world. In other words, a world in which people could maintain secrets more easily and where private agonies were beyond easy public scrutiny. It had to be a world and place in which people from very different backgrounds would meet and fall in love. After many hours sitting in cafés staring at nothing in particular while running different scenarios in my head, hours of research and sifting through my own memories of half-understood scandals whispered by grown-ups when I was young, and my own misspent late teens, about 1970 seemed to be the right time frame. Ireland, along with much of the world, was going through a great social upheaval then. Hippies, drugs, free love, sex, and rock and roll had swept up on the Irish shores and made their way to the youth in even small villages, though it may have been in a more sedate way than in bigger cities. So, there was the nub of it. It had to be a village, somewhere a young

Irish woman could feel the lure of liberation enough to embark on a relationship outside her class with an already married older man, and yet, a place where it was possible to be discreet enough to hide it.

After a lot more staring into space and research, I finally settled on the fact that the story needed two time frames to work. One was the 1970s; the other, 1990s. Paternity tests had to be reliable and used, the internet not widely available, and cell phones non-existent. Abortion laws in various places had to be researched. Research informed me that Scotland issued an automatic short form birth certificate when a birth was registered. This short form only gave details about the person registered and not their parents, so that, together with access to adoption information available to adoptees, caused a hasty move for one of my characters from Wales to Scotland. What I uncovered meant a major rethink of part of the story as I conceived it. All that done, I was down to deciding on the actual location of these characters. Much as I would love to say I had all this worked out before I began to write, that would be untrue. I did not. I noted a few key scenes that the story needed and began to write. It was only when the inevitable question of how and where the two main characters met arose that I grappled with creating the actual village where the story took place. To come alive to me, the village, first of all, had to have a name.

Every district in Ireland pretty much has a Big House. That is where the relatively wealthy Anglo-Irish family lived. The gentry, in other words. Though they lived within the village or town vicinity, the Big House residents weren't quite part of the village. Villagers knew this, and so did the gentry. Their paths would cross, and both parties would be polite and friendly, but social mixing didn't happen very much. It wasn't inconceivable that the story I wanted to tell may have happened one way or another in a number of these environments. Or some version of unsuitable liaisons anyway, and so I didn't want to set it in a village that actually existed. Another round of research began.

I must have spent about three hours one evening thinking up names for an imaginary Irish village. Every darn one I tried, no matter how improbable it seemed to me, already existed. Many Irish city, town, and village names are Anglo impositions from the original Irish name. For example, quite a number of places are Bally-something-or-other, e.g.: Ballygreen, Ballyconnell, etc. Originally their names started *Baile na*, which means "place of" in proper translation. In part, because it's misused in so many non-Irish books, plays, and movies, I didn't want to use Bally, and as I clearly wasn't able to come up with an Irish-sounding name that wasn't already a real place, I did what I always do if I am writing or editing at home and get stuck. I found some small corner of my place that needed cleaning or tidying and set about doing that. The task was done while not actively thinking about the writing problem I wanted to solve; instead, the answer came while my hands were busy and my mind was on, what I call, 'free roam.' In this state, all sorts of stuff floats through my mind — bits of songs, odd memories, irritation that I hadn't attended to whatever task I'd set myself sooner — while vaguely keeping the writing problem in sight, though not actively thinking about it. Invariably a solution would pop up, and the task would be abandoned — think of the chaos of half-finished tasks in my place. On second thoughts, don't. And, so, it did this time. I resolved to move on to another distinctly Irish type of name Kil-something, as in Kilkee, Kilkenny. Kil, or sometimes Kill, is another Anglo word from the Irish *cill*, which means church. However, my imagination had no more luck finding a unique name with the prefix Kil. Another hour of trying, and I'd had enough. It was back to the task of cleaning and tidying.

This time a memory drifted into my mind. When I first moved to the city as a child, we had a local shop (corner store to Canadians) not very far from our house. Every day a farmer from out the road came by with a few churns of fresh milk settled into the back of his horse and trap. These were delivered to the shop, and empty churns were taken away. Folks who wanted to buy milk brought a container to the store, asked for how much they wanted (a pint, half-pint, quart etc.), and it was ladled with a marked measure into their container. At the end, a little bit extra, called a tilly, was ladled in too. My family had a proper milk can with a wire handle and lid. Not long after our move, milk was delivered in bottles with tinfoil caps, and our milk can was relegated to storage. That is until my Dad had to spend some time in bed. I don't remember whether it was because he was ill or because of some surgery he'd had, but getting out of bed was a problem for him. Making his way to the bathroom (no en suites in our house), was out of the question. He needed a chamber pot. The only one we had, a lovely porcelain thing, was already assigned to my grandmother, who lived with us in a downstairs room and, thus, was in much more need of a chamber pot than Da. Something had to be found. The milk can was back in use. My Da named the milk can Tilly. When that popped into my head, I knew I had my village name. A quick computer search confirmed it. There was no city, town, or village in Ireland called Kiltilly.

Filling the town with houses and establishments and specific locations was easy after that. I simply moved buildings and whole roads that I knew to one imaginary town of Kiltilly. The hospital where my main characters met and the square where the bus left for towns and cities come from my mother's village, where I spent part of all the summers of my childhood with my aunts. The places exist, though I've taken liberties with them, I'm afraid. A favourite walk of mine from the city limit to where I lived in a cottage in the country was moved a few dozen miles from its original location on one side of Limerick city to the imaginary village of Kiltilly on the other. I even shuffled time and incorporated a lovely little café that does exist in the village square, but the café wasn't there until much, much later than the 1990s. And the proprietor is much warmer and less intrusive than that the one in story.

By drawing on favourite memories, places I knew well, and customs and behaviours I observed keenly as a young person, I was able to create a place for my characters to inhabit. A place that became almost real to me as I wrote. What thrills me most about *Left Unsaid* now is that people ask me where in Ireland Kiltilly is. It is everywhere and nowhere.

PROMPT:

Setting is integral to characters in a story. Mostly we think of setting as a particular place, yet it is more than that. Besides living in a particular place, our characters live in a particular time or social setting, which has as much influence on them as the actual physical place they live.

Introduce a character with one sentence as they wrestle with a problem relating to their social position or a social restraint they are under because of the time they live in or circumstances of their life (it can be a long or short sentence). Then describe where they are physically (a room, a house, a castle, a field, a boardroom, or even what they're wearing) and add one or two details that indicate either their social position or a social constraint they are under. In the end, and only then, come back to the character.

ART INSPIRED WRITING

CANDIE TANAKA

As a writer and artist, art inspires and informs my writing through storytelling with visual imagery, objects, and sounds in many different ways. When I go to galleries, museums, outdoor spaces, libraries, peer into artist catalogues and books, visit artist studios, talk to artists, or view work online, I will notice linguistic inspiration in art. This intermedial creative process in contemporary literary studies is actually referred to as ekphrasis. Producing words in this way has become a key aspect of my writing practice. There is a connection between neuroscience and cognitive science in our brains when the process of ekphrasis occurs.

When I use a camera, which is a quicker route to access some imagery, I may choose to use the frame as a container of visual language. I'm reframing objects in a picture, just as I would move words around in a sentence. I'm constructing a story that has yet to be written. An image that I've created can inspire memories or return me to the exact time and place where I can feel the warmth and sense the kindness of friends or lovers, taste the food, hear the music, and feel the raw emotions of love, regret, and tenderness. Photography is this kind of mechanical reproduction that can trigger visual thinking that then prompts me to describe an image in words. Photographer Robert Frank once said, "When people look at my pictures I want them to feel the way they do when they want to read a line of a poem twice."

When I research writing about place, I will sometimes take dozens and dozens of digital photographs with both my DSLR camera and my phone because some of the distant spaces may not be easy to return to. But place doesn't just consist of a physical space, it can also include sounds, smells, language, customs, culture, and values. This process is done with the full understanding that I will, at some point later, most likely, translate this imagery into words for a story. Sometimes I don't realize this right away when I'm taking photos, but I'm not just keeping them as images; I'm building a story as photojournalists do, but mine will be strictly text based. When I want to return to those spaces in my writing, I will initially try to imagine them in a non-direct way without a digital image. Then, I will search for the photo on my computer, look at it, and close my eyes and imagine I'm back there, experiencing all of its dimensions at that moment when the image was first captured. There are actually ten possible dimensions when looking at the universe using string theory. Aside from the standard four dimensions, X, Y, Z and time, the rest are considered possible worlds, such as all possible futures or all possible pasts in all of their alternate realities. Some of these are so tiny and fleeting that we have no way of detecting them at the present time.

The biggest challenge for me in writing my first manuscript was genre. I had started working on a non-fiction novel using a memoir style of writing. I was laying down factual experiences of the lives of my Japanese Canadian grandparents on my father's side of the family. I thought more about historical bias in communities and the challenges around individual and collective memory. My family's story is missing from the narrative of the Japanese Canadian community in Vancouver because of historical documents in a folder that my aunt had been holding onto. These were objects that very few had ever seen and contained stories that happened during the internment with my father's family and their community of neighbours and friends. My writing around this new information had originally started off as a short story, but as I progressed further along, through research and various iterations, I could eventually feel the shape of it changing. The structure and style of my writing were going off on a different tangent, and rather than try to contain it, I let it go, and it moved me towards working in fiction. Some of this, in a roundabout way, was also due to viewing Niki de Saint Phalle's large colourful outdoor sculptures and Yoko Ono's conceptual art of word paintings. I used these as examples during the writing of my novel and wanted to bring those lexicons of colour, simplicity, and daydreams into the direction that my manuscript was going. Throughout my research, as I crafted the story, I began taking on the role of an unreliable narrator, of sorts, as well, telling myself the story from a third-person perspective but filling in the gaps with my own thoughts or conjecture.

Once, on an overseas trip years ago, I decided to go to an island that was quite the ferry journey to get to. There, I visited a gallery full of sounds. There was a long corridor that you could walk through that was filled with sonic art. After I stepped out from the exhibition and away from the venue, the experience evoked all kinds of emotions. I was on the sand facing the ocean, and I looked across the water, wanting to reach out arms across the horizon for someone that I loved. The day was a moody grey, and I could feel the sounds and motion of the waves as they made tiny indelible marks against my heart. I thought of the words and the love that had become a vocabulary for my aural experience and then the syntax that would best shape and hold this audio, then placed them into a story. Some of this would be indicated by silence on the page or through awkward conversation between characters. And at other times, the sounds would play out in my dreams. After that, I was ready to delineate and rework the words in my notebook, then place them into a stronger narrative. Listening in arts spaces with open ears is a big part of my writing, and when I do that, the words will reward me with clarity.

When I do have an opportunity to visit local galleries, I like to make sure that I don't always go to the same spaces that everyone goes to and definitely not the same exhibits everyone sees. This is because I don't want to write or think about the same experiences as everyone else. When I'm near home in Vancouver, I also enjoy a few of the smaller galleries and exhibits in Chinatown, such as at 221A, Access Gallery, Canton-sardine, and Centre A or ones nearby, like the grunt gallery, CSA Space, or Artspeak, where mini-groups of viewers attend an artist talk. Oftentimes, I will see art in unexpected spaces, like laboratories, storage units, libraries, nature reserves, hotels, sheds, kitchens, or alleyways. I like to go to see things that other people don't go to. It allows me to talk about experiences in my writing that others may have missed. I usually like to be in spaces where there are few other people so I can view the art in silence. With smaller artists' talks, too, you have an opportunity to connect with people through words who are there because they are interested in the topic. Some of my favourite works of sculpture are outdoors, not so much in this city, but in other places that I've had an opportunity to visit. Once at a gallery or an art space, I engage with it, using all of my senses. Art is a perception of time that can take you rapidly back in centuries or to another space entirely. Galleries and other art spaces create dialogical room for me to share and reflect on my personal thoughts about the art. I like to build a kind of collective dialogue, challenge my values, participate in calls to action, and learn from other artists. My lines of text are messy mark-making, and the art I prefer layers works over other works that sometimes blur together in different dimensions. At points, I will make an entirely new work out of words that might be somewhat related. Art spaces, too, are where I have experienced the most intense love that I have ever felt for other people. These relationships may have lasted years or only for the duration of a gallery visit, but they've always been memorable, and these emotions I've also brought into my writing practice.

Art is always political, and that's what I love about it. I like to look through art journals, magazines, artist compilations, and art history books. There, I notice words, phrases, and images outside my usual vernacular. I like to then bring this language or way of seeing with me into my writing. Some great examples of political work include Kara Walker's critique of colonialism and her forty-two-foot-high sculpture *Fons Americanus* at the Tate Modern, Ai Weiwei's work and its criticism of the Chinese Government's human rights and democracy positions, or Yoko Ono and her anti-war stance. Art makes parallels with what's happening in world history and how an artist can interpret their own positionality.

Art is my writing companion and is always ever-present in my work. It's helped me to develop critical thinking skills so that I can better articulate thoughts and concepts around creative processes. I like to disrupt my narrative by tearing it apart and putting it back together again, looking inside and digging deep to make meaning, and then picking at it and pulling out the words or ideas that I can then use in my writing.

PROMPT:
Sit in an art gallery for fifteen minutes. Bring a notebook or sketch-book, and make marks or words about one or two pieces that resonate with you. After you leave the space, write a short story or a poem about your experience in the next few days.

A CHARACTER IS NOT AN ISLAND: CREATING CHARACTER NETWORKS

MARIA REVA

Give your character a desire. Give them a quirk, a job, a limp or a tic, a backstory, credit card debt. Search their purses and backpacks for clues about their personhood. Ponder that ChapStick flavor.

Early on in my writing practice, whenever an instructor or guidebook prompted me to develop my characters via a laundry list of traits and possessions, I would invariably get stuck. While fellow students unearthed entire backstories using only Tic Tac boxes or keychain flashlights as clues, I could not. Unable to bring myself to care about my characters' purse content, I thought I lacked heart and — worst of all — imagination. Wasn't a "real" writer supposed to spin story from just about anything, like Rumpelstiltskin spinning gold from straw? From the stories I'd written by that point, I *still* didn't know my protagonists' every preference, allergy, or whether they required a sleep mask or blackout curtains at night.

A few years into my foray into fiction, I began working on a linked story collection set in an apartment block in Soviet Ukraine. Perhaps it was the setting of the book — the enforced communality of the political system, the fact of entire extended families cramped into tiny suites — that taught me that it was okay to consider characters as part of a dense social network before I could get to know them as individuals. In fact, if I let myself think of each character as a lone actor puttering along to fulfil their individual needs and goals, the narrative tension would grow slack. It was the dynamics *between* the characters that interested me the most. Yes, by the last draft of a story, I did have a sense of who each character was — their temperament, "aura," "energy," "soul," whatever you want to call it — but this gradual discovery was a by-product of another exploration: what do the characters need from *each other*? Who has power over whom? Who knows something the other doesn't? How does this taut network of needs, desires, power, and knowledge shift when a new character is thrown into the mix?

What is individuality anyway? A North American ideal, certainly, which bleeds into how we approach characterisation in fiction. But what intrigues me most about individuality: is it ossified, unyielding? Or is it ever-shifting, depending on the environment and who else is in the room? Depending on who our protagonist is trying to win over, impress?

The closer I can keep character needs and desires within a network, the more potential I have for tension in my stories. For example, if my protagonist must go to the dentist for a complex procedure, they could go to a character who has no consequence in the story beyond that dental visit, or they could go to the ex-lover we've already met — who is also the best dentist in town. Consider the potential for tension in that visit: the protagonist is desperate to have their dental woes fixed but must face the person with whom they share a turbulent past.

Liz Feldman's darkly comedic show *Dead to Me* is a great example of a tight-knit, tension-filled character network. (Apologies for spoilers.) The show opens with a woman named Jen joining a grief therapy group after her husband gets killed in a hit-and-run. She becomes close with one of the group members, an affable woman named Judy. Widow Jen soon invites New Friend Judy, who is going through a divorce, to move in with her and her kids. We soon find out that it is New Friend Judy who was driving the car that had hit Widow Jen's husband (Widow Jen herself does not yet know this). This is why guilt-ridden New Friend Judy desperately wanted to befriend Widow

Jen: to help her in any way she could without actually confessing. New Friend Judy even joins Widow Jen in her hit-and-run investigation. Note that the driver of the hit-and-run could have been some random person we've never meet, someone off-screen. But isn't it more suspenseful and emotionally complex to have the driver be a character we've already grown to love? Widow Jen's goal (to find the person who hit her husband) is in direct conflict with New Friend Judy's goal (to get away with it, and yet still assuage her guilty conscience).

Note, as well, the asymmetry of power and knowledge between the two women: New Friend Judy comes to rely on Widow Jen for a stable home. Widow Jen relies on New Friend Judy for the kind of companionship she's never had before. New Friend Judy holds the key to Widow Jen's search for her husband's killer. If Widow Jen finds out it was New Friend Judy, she could destroy her best friend's life — and that's a lot of power, yet untapped.

Further on in the season, when Widow Jen and New Friend Judy attend a grief retreat, New Friend Judy develops a fling with another retreat attendee. She soon finds out that that man is a detective who is currently on leave. She asks the detective how hit-and-run investigations are conducted to better understand how she can get away with hers. She ends up telling him about the hit-and-run that killed Widow Jen's husband. New Friend Judy's questions lead him to begin secretly investigating this hit-and-run himself. He soon figures out that New Friend Judy was the one behind the wheel. Note that New Friend Judy's love interest could have any other occupation — a landscape architect or a veterinarian. Instead, his occupation directly connects to the main drama of the show, the hit-and-run investigation. He is at first an ally to New Friend Judy, unwittingly helping her get away with her crime, before becoming an obstacle by trying to get her arrested. He thus becomes deeply embedded in the show's character network.

The characters in *Dead to Me* don't just have individual desires. They are dependent on one another to fill those desires and needs.

Their actions impact the character network and connect to the central question of the show's first season: will Widow Jen find out that her best friend was the one who killed her husband? This makes for a season wrought with suspense.

(To note: amassing an inventory of autobiographical details can indeed be useful; your character's background informs narrative voice and worldview. Choice of ChapStick flavour — Organic Pumpkin Spice Cozy Delight vs. Unscented Petroleum — can give the reader an insight into character. But if details like these don't come "naturally" to you as a writer, fear not. You aren't unimaginative or uncaring.)

Character networks can be both a generative and diagnostic tool. You might map out how your characters relate to one another on a sheet of paper or white board before beginning your story. Or you might write multiple drafts without any outlines or maps, plopping your characters into the same room to see how they fare. If, in the latter case, you find your tension lagging, try mapping out the character network you already have. Is there a character on the sidelines who can be reeled in closer to the central question of the story, or should that character be retired from the story? Is there a power or knowledge differential that could be tapped? Remember, every time your character has a need, this creates the opportunity for another character to be an ally or obstacle. Which will it be? Your reader will have to turn the page to find out.

PROMPT:
Amanita and Igor work at the same company. Amanita witnesses Igor doing something he shouldn't, something that could harm the company. Let's imagine three scenarios:

1. Amanita is superior to Igor (she's his boss).
2. Amanita is equal to Igor.
3. Amanita is inferior to Igor (he's her boss).

For each scenario, write a short scene (one hundred words) in which Amanita confronts Igor about his wrongdoing. Does the power dynamic affect how each scene plays out? What do the characters need/desire from one another, and how does this change between your three scenes? Which of your three scenes is the most suspenseful, tense?

SO YOU WANT TO WRITE ABOUT RACE

JEN SOOKFONG LEE

Somehow, I have become an expert on writing race.

This was not something I planned for. When I started publishing, I was writing fiction about Chinese Canadian characters, about families who had been invisible in CanLit, not because of politics, really, but because it was a story I knew I could write that also hadn't been told yet. I was twenty-three years old (the same age as any random TikTok star!) when I started *The End of East*, and my politics were ill-formed and likely carelessly considered. When the novel was published, I was unprepared for how much people wanted me to talk about race: about other Asian authors, about immigration, about diversity in publishing, even about the effects of Chinese investment on Canadian real estate prices (not a topic I enjoy, so I have since stopped trying to engage). After a few months of promoting *The End of East*, I developed stock answers that were designed to both deflect attention from my race and to make people laugh. My favourite? Whenever someone at an event asked what the Chinese Canadian community thought of my book, I would answer, "There are 1.5 million of us, and I haven't had time to talk to everyone. But I'm pretty sure at least half a dozen think it sucks."

Thirteen years and nine books later, I have come to an uneasy peace about my position as The Accessible Inclusion Lady of CanLit, influenced, at least partly, by the number of young writers of colour who write or talk to me at events, asking if they will ever get published, if there is a place for them in our industry. The anxiety they articulate is very real, and their awareness of how imbalanced the book business can be is acute, far more so than mine at the same career stage.

My visibility, I've come to learn, is important for them. My willingness to speak about representation matters to them. For this reason, the space I've been given to speak about race and appropriation and diversity is one that I'm happy to occupy, even if I sometimes don't want to, even if I would rather be asked about my craft or research or how much I will always love *Possession* by A.S. Byatt. This space means I have influence, that my knowledge holds power, and this is a privilege that I do not take for granted.

(And I should say that not everyone who is asked to represent a community needs to or should. Some prefer to let their literary work speak for their politics. Others would rather leave all of that alone. That's all good!)

But what do I say when someone asks, "But Jen, how do I write about race when it's not my race?"

This is a question I've been asked hundreds of times, usually by emerging writers, but also sometimes by established ones who are now wrestling with the idea that writing race requires some measure of accountability. And it isn't always white writers asking either. It can be easy to assume that appropriation only flows in one direction — white writers taking on the stories of BIPOC. This assumption, though, centres on whiteness inaccurately. Writers from all communities are worried about appropriation and representation because everyone wants their writing to reflect the reality of our lives. Diversity is a fact of our cities, workplaces, and media, with or without whiteness.

When someone asks how they can write about race, a part of me is tempted to respond with, "Would you ever ask Dave Eggers this question?" But in truth, this is a topic I take very seriously, for emerging writers, but also for my own work.

Whenever I start a writing project, when the premise is forming, and I'm starting to write down ideas or an outline, I always refer to, what I call, my Cultural Checklist. As I move through drafts and revisions, I look through the list again and again, to keep my brain on track.

CULTURAL CHECKLIST

1. **Question your idea**. Before you get started, ask yourself, "Am I the person to write this story?" So often, problems arise when writers try to tell stories that are strongly and identifiably tied to specific communities. Are you the person who should be writing a story about residential schools, or internment, or refugee camps? Can you tell this story with more or less authority than someone from that community? If you're writing non-fiction, can you make space for a person to tell their own story? Can this be part of your structure? If it's fiction, can you find a path into that story that feels authentic to you, without taking on the voice of someone else? And are you writing about a community that has less privilege than yours when you could be helping that community tell their own stories instead?

2. **Give your characters space**, whether they are your protagonist or your supporting characters. A diverse cast of characters is great! It's ideal! But take care to identify your characters with other markers, not just race. Every character, no matter how secondary, deserves enough space to be the hero in their own stories, even if those stories are only one paragraph long. Hint at their backstories. Tell us how they're acting and what they're wearing. Make sure we know them as something other than That [insert race here] Person.

3. **Refer to race without stating race**. When I finished reading *Brother* by David Chariandy, what struck me was that his characters were young men from all kinds of families, but he did not identify their race to us. Instead, he described what kinds of haircuts they had, or what they cooked, or gave them names from a specific lan-

guage. In this way, we knew what their race was, but these markers gave us more than race; they gave us genuinely interesting details that helped us get to know these characters better than just race ever could.

4. **Approach your characters as you would a human in real life**. Whenever we meet people at a party or in line at Starbucks, we start conversations with generosity and understand that we begin not knowing anything about them, and that the process of familiarity is full of surprises we can never anticipate. This is the same for your fictional characters too. Real humans will never conform to a stereotype or a fetish, and our characters shouldn't either. How will they surprise you? What will you discover about them that is delightful, or disturbing, or challenging?

5. **Do the work**. It really comes down to research, finding the right sensitivity readers, and constantly questioning your narrative decisions. It's important to conduct as much research as you can before approaching a sensitivity reader because you want to be as specific as possible. For example, if your book is set in a small farming town in Syria, finding a reader who knows about agriculture from the region is more precise and helpful than simply finding someone of Syrian descent. Writing a book is always an exercise in hard work, in doing more than you thought you could. Race, like dialogue or setting or plot, requires time, revision, and a critical eye.

We can and should write what lights a fire in our bellies, but the issue of appropriation allows us to consider how our writing will be seen in the world. How will agents or editors read our characters? How will readers feel about our use of race or culture? The last thing we want as authors is for our readers to be bounced out of our stories because a detail or a reference isn't right or feels exploitative.

Here are some practical exercises for all stages of the writing process that you can try to help you address any appropriation issues.

1. Write a piece of flash fiction in the voice of your childhood best friend, in their home, with their family. Do not stop to research any details, such as names of foods, languages, or places of origin, but instead use whatever detail you think might be accurate. Once you're done, circle all the details you had to guess and research them. How accurate were you? What did you get wrong? Can you apply this same editing eye to your main project?

2. Take one community from your writing project, and read a book from a member of that community. Be as specific as possible with identity markers, including geography, ethnic identity, sexuality, and gender. As you're reading, make note of every detail about this culture you didn't know. Is it more or less than you thought?

3. Identify one character from your writing project who isn't like you. Choose one of their main characteristics (maybe they are a serial monogamist, or obsessed with accumulating wealth, or a very bad dancer). Using what you've learned from research, connect their background to their characteristic. Ask yourself if it's a direct linear connection (e.g.: they grew up in poverty within a remote and under-serviced rural community and are now determined to earn as much as possible), or a circuitous emotional one, or a connection inspired by their desire to distance themselves from their origins. Write the story of that connection.

As you embark on your writing project with all of this in mind, I want you to ask yourself one more question: can you make space for writers from marginalized communities to tell their own stories? Buy a book from an emerging writer of colour. Attend a reading featuring someone whose work is new to you. Amplify their work on your social media channels. After all, accountability doesn't stop when you've written what you want. Accountability extends to creating opportunities for everyone. Life, like the best fiction, is expansive, diverse, and cacophonous. Embrace that. It's a beautiful thing. I'm The Accessible Inclusion Lady of CanLit. You can trust me.

THE FIVE THINGS COUNSELLING CAN TEACH US ABOUT WRITING AND CHARACTER DEVELOPMENT

EILEEN COOK

I grew up with practical parents. While they supported my plan of becoming a writer, they also wisely advised that I should have a way to support myself. Given that I am a big fan of things like eating and shelter, I agreed. When I reviewed my skills, I knew I was someone that other people went to when they had a question or problem, so counselling seemed a reasonable target.

In addition to providing me with a living until I could write full-time, counselling gave me the opportunity to study human behaviour. I discovered that writers can learn a lot from counsellors, that they can help us create better characters and more realistic responses to conflict and crisis, making our books richer and deeper.

Here are the five things writers can learn from counsellors:

1. Take a non-judgmental approach:
Counsellors are trained to approach people with an open and empathetic response. It doesn't mean that the counsellor doesn't have a personal opinion about whatever the individual may be struggling with, but rather it means that when working with them, we maintain a balanced approach. The goal of counselling is, of course, to assist people, not judge them.

What does this mean for writers?

It means remembering that all people are making the best choice in the moment with the knowledge and ability that they have. This doesn't mean that it's a good choice (Lord knows some characters/ people make some really questionable ones), only that they're doing the best they can. As the author or creator, you need to have empathy and understanding for what your characters are doing if you want readers to connect with those characters.

Your main character and the supporting cast will be under pressure in the book. You may be killing off people important to them, burning down their business, or crashing an asteroid into their planet. When people are under stress, they don't always respond in the best way. If you know the core of who your characters are, it will be easier to understand how they will respond in different circumstances; and it will be easier for the reader to understand how the character's goals and motivations move them forward.

The villains in your story have their own goals and motivations, after all, they don't know they're the bad guy. As far as they're concerned, they're the hero. When writing your antagonists, steer away from easy answers — that they're doing something bad because they're just bad people, or worse, that they're doing something bad because you need them to for the purpose of the plot.

2. Listen to what is said:

Counselling is fundamentally the art of listening. Often in human interaction, we're thinking of what we're going to say in response before the person has even finished speaking. Counselling means truly attending to what the other individual is saying and the words they choose to express themselves.

What does this mean for writers?

Don't rush to shove words into your characters' mouths. Think about what they want to communicate and the words they'd choose to express themselves. This word choice is likely impacted by both their level of education (ambulate versus walk, periwinkle versus blue) and, also, by what emotion they're feeling as they're trying to express themselves. We're writers; if there's anything we should know, it's that words matter. Think about what words your character would choose and how who they are talking to impacts that communication.

3. Listen to what is not said:

Counsellors pay attention not only to what the client says but also to what *isn't* said. While we hope that everyone is aware and has insight into their own motivations and beliefs, the reality is that most of us are still working that out. (No wonder there is so much job security in counselling!)

Individuals may not know what they feel or may not know how to best express it. Counsellors are skilled at reading non-verbal behaviour. Does the individual lean forward or back when talking? Are their arms crossed over their chest? Jaw clenched? Picking at their finger-nails? Counsellors are looking at how a client's actions can tell them more about what may be going on inside that person. Do their actions match what they are saying, or is it in contrast?

What does this mean for writers?

In filmmaking, there's the term used to describe dialogue as "on the nose." This term is used to describe dialogue where the spoken words are exactly what the character is thinking or feeling. It feels off to the listener because it's too honest for the situation. The truth is that most of us aren't that honest in our communication.

As a writer, you may also have your characters being too in-touch with what they think and feel. Readers enjoy being a part of the storytelling process. When you provide them with clues, they're able to unravel the complexities of your story with you. For example, if you have this in your manuscript: *"Why John, I would love nothing more than to go out with you tonight," Kelly said, twisting the rings on her fingers.* As a reader, I see that ring twisting as telling. It makes me think that, perhaps, she's not quite as excited about this date as she seems to be implying, that she might be nervous or have a secret that she's keeping from John. Raising those questions, and intriguing the reader, is exactly what keeps them turning pages! Pay as much attention to what your characters don't say — and the body language they use — as to what comes out of their mouth.

4. Be curious about human behaviour:

Fundamentally, counsellors are intrigued with other people and their actions and how to assist people with the challenges they face. There is an ever-growing base of information on what motivates people and how people respond in a variety of life situations.

What does this mean for writers?

If you've been looking only in writing craft books for advice on how to deepen your characters or to make them more realistic, then you're missing a huge section of your library or local bookstore. The self-help section is a treasure trove of character details. Consider the issues your character may have, from past addiction to PTSD, to grief, to loving too much (or too little), to struggling with a difficult child — I guarantee there's a book that explores this in detail. Many of these books contain case studies and examples that may spark your imagination. These exercises or suggestions may provide you with a road map of how your character could move through those changes.

5. Believe that people can change:

Counsellors are optimists. They believe that people can, and do, make changes in their lives — especially when they're committed to those changes. However, counsellors also understand that change is difficult. Most individuals don't change because it's much easier to stay in our current patterns.

What does this mean for writers?

Your character likely needs to make a change over the course of the book as they reach for their goal or desire in the story. They may need to learn to be a part of a team, to trust others, or to believe in themselves. Are you making it difficult for them to make that change? Do they try and fail? If they aren't failing at least once, you haven't made the goal difficult enough for them.

Writers, like counsellors, are fascinated by human behavior and choice. Taking a counselling approach, and putting your characters on the spot, will help you understand their motivations more deeply and create realistic responses to events in the story that will keep readers turning pages.

PROMPT:

Pretend that your main character (also, perhaps, your antagonist) has come to you for counselling. What do they see as their problem? How do they express themselves? What events happened in their life before this that impact how they see the world? What non-verbal behaviours do you see — do they match their words? What advice would you give them to move forward?

STEPPING INTO PERSPECTIVE

JOANNE BETZLER

Twenty-odd years ago, I learned from my son that his friend's brother had died by suicide. At the victim's funeral, I wept and pictured his mother's face as the minister read her poem of lost hopes and dreams for her child, her longing to turn back the clock, to slay his demons. For weeks, the simple act of breathing became laboured and my eyes an unpredictable font as I tried to make sense of a boy's tragedy. A boy I'd never even met.

What demons drove this child to his death? How could his parents, sibling, grandparents, possibly survive such a nightmare? How could his friends, his teachers cope? How could his mother go on?

How could any mother go on?

What if it was my child...

Over time, the intensity of my feelings quieted, but they never disappeared. Survivor stories followed me everywhere, and their persistent chatter became fragments of a novel trapped in my head. Twenty years later, these fragments became the natural choice for my project in the Writer's Studio, and I wrote what I saw from the naivety of my imagination.

Sharing my writing was new, and I felt nervous at the prospect of discussing it with near-strangers, but I was committed to the program and to myself as a writer. My early submissions of a family torn apart by the pain of suicide tugged on a few heartstrings and received encouraging comments from some of my group. For others, shock and disbelief blocked their acceptance. But the single, skeptical challenge "What *is* this?" made my ears burn and my heart race.

This story had dogged me for over two decades. Paying equal respect to the pain of each person connected to the victim was the right approach. Wasn't it?

A consult with my mentor Hiromi Goto, helped me recognize the folly of trying to elicit empathy for an entire community of people. Such broad focus could only result in a slurry of character emotions to confuse the reader. She pointed out the need for consistent point of view (POV): omniscient, first, second, or third. All deserved consideration. Her suggestion that I choose three to five characters, get to know them, and tell their stories from their own perspectives, sounded daunting to my untrained writer's brain. But, the handful of novels using multiple character POVs she recommended opened my eyes.

This time, my increased heart rate told me: I could fix this.

Because I sympathized with the pain of an entire community, it was difficult enough to narrow my character pool to five, let alone three, but the prospect of befriending each character fed my enthusiasm. Which handful was closest to the suicide victim and had the most to lose by his death? Should I include the victim himself? Instinct told me the estranged dad belonged in a supporting role, so I focussed on the troubled teenager, his mother, his little sister, his big brother, and his brother's friend.

Each one was assigned a poster-sized sheet of cardboard where I recorded details as I came to know them better. What did they like, want, need, fear, and so on, and would those traits change over the story arc? These character charts of my core cast helped me clarify and embrace their uniqueness. I could pick each one up, like a needy child, and give it my undivided attention.

And I began my rewrite. Starting with the victim's older brother, choosing past tense, omniscient POV, I watched over his actions and reactions from his perspective. I could picture his will, his pain, and his connections to the other characters. He became almost real.

Except reality is subjective. My peers applauded the changes and growth, but to my frustration, still found my character and his story wanting. Emotionally deficient, questionable authenticity, lacking depth were a few of the comments.

Hiromi's feedback again helped me regroup. What if I maintained past tense but changed the narrative to the first person? Rather than observe my characters, I'd step into their minds to see what they saw and feel what they felt.

Hmm. Maybe…

Since the female psyches would be easiest for me to connect with, I'd test the theory on the victim's twelve-year-old sister. Already familiar with her athletic interests, friends, and family frustrations, the change of pronouns from *she* and *her* to *I* and *me* felt comfortable. I summoned my forgotten middle-school mindset of pre-teen angst to tweak the narrative from inside her head and help me understand her individuality.

I decided to tackle the boys next. To mirror the male teenage consciousness, I imagined myself in their places and consulted a handful of trustworthy males who read my work and offered constructive feedback. To get close and pay respect to the Indo-Canadian family friend's POV, I took detailed notes of my many discussions and feedback from supportive members of that community.

As their credibility grew, my characters began following me. Not just their stories. Themselves, popping into my life, all demanding I listen and get it right.

The first time I sat on the 128 bus, at its 3:00 p.m. stop in front of the high school, I heard the victim's older brother bantering with his friends. I sat up straight and listened. When I witnessed his younger sister ignoring her mother's lecture at the grocery checkout, I watched closely. And walking my dog through the neighbourhood, I often sensed the victim's mother alongside me, deep in thought.

With every one of their unpredictable appearances, I became adept at recording notes on my phone. And because of their random visits on television, in books, in the newspaper, or in my sleep, a pad of sticky notes and a pen became fixtures beside my chair and my bed.

As I witnessed their hopes, pain and anger, reactions, and behaviours, they blended into my own life. First-person POV helped me unweave their personalities and appreciate who was identifiable and who was less willing to be recognized. I honed my key character pool to three: the victim's mother, brother, and sister. The deceased boy, while key to the unfolding narrative, was unreachable in any way but memory. And his brother's Indo-Canadian friend was beyond my scope of experience. Much loved by all characters, this friend became the broken family's link.

Once my year at TWS ended, peer feedback came from my biweekly writers' group. Always supportive and helpful, they were enthusiastic about my use of first-person POV. After one session discussing a chapter from the sister's perspective, two or three participants said they liked her a lot but still felt slightly removed from her. What if, instead of looking back and imagining what was, I switched to the present tense?

Hmm. Write in the moment... Why not?

What is a mom's reaction to finding her son dead in the basement? How does she survive? What does a twelve-year-old sister imagine when she arrives home to police cars, their lights flashing in front of her house? How does a seventeen-year-old react when he learns about his brother's death from his best friend because his mom is unable to think clearly? Did I really want to know?

Of course I did. I needed to get this right.

I began the process with a new chapter of the brother's journey, knowing the exact point to which he was headed and all the stops he'd make along the way. Embracing the teen's loss and his anger, I wrote. Barely one paragraph in, images, words, and phrases consumed my consciousness. Time and space vanished as the narrative adopted a will of its own and pulled me along an unexpected path, then stopped.

What just happened? I shook the fog from my head, turned to my monitor, and read.

What the heck? Eight hundred words, not remotely what I'd planned to write when I'd sat down. But it worked. Somehow my character knew from the start where he'd wanted to go and had taken me there himself.

Who knew writing could be so exhilarating?

It happened again with the sister and again with the mother. Each time I gave myself over to their immediacy, they stepped up to steer the narrative and take me places I'd never fathom until we arrived.

I'd expected the task of stepping into my characters' skins — feeling the brother's fury, the mother's despair, and the daughter's life-altering nightmare — to be visceral and exhausting. Instead, I felt enlightened and liberated. My characters had heart. Minds of their own. I could trust their voices. Now, when I recall the reactions of my TWS cohort to my early submissions, I get it. How could anyone possibly believe in my characters until I believed in them myself?

The catharsis has extended beyond my writing. I am at peace with my relentless scenarios of suicide and grief. They may not be gone but now reside in a small pocket of my long-term memory, waiting for their next call to fiction.

PROMPT:
Once I'd been coaxed out from my naïve assumption that past tense third-person omniscient was my only POV choice, my mind opened to understand the value of assessing options to select the best perspective for specific manuscripts.

Try this:
- Select a key scene or section of your work involving your main character, and, using the past tense, write it in third-person omniscient.
- Take the same scene and, maintaining past tense, rewrite it in the first person POV of that same character.
- Retaining first-person POV, change the same scene to present tense.

How do the shifts in immediacy, objectivity, emotion, and closeness impact the overall power of the scene? Does one resonate more strongly than the others? Choose the perspective that speaks to you and best conveys the spirit of your story.

POINT OF VIEW: THE STRUGGLE IS REAL

JANIE CHANG

I remember quite vividly the moment when I realized point of view (POV) would be an issue.

As a hesitant first step toward writing a novel, I was taking "Fiction Series for the Weekend Student," a Continuing Studies course taught by the wonderful Caroline Adderson at Simon Fraser University. Most of my classmates were at least twenty years younger and, from the way they dressed, had been born with the scarf-tying gene. It was also clear they'd taken creative writing courses before, tossing around terms such as "postmodernism" (which I confused with post-Impressionism). Then a young man with floppy hair (and an artfully knotted scarf) raised his hand to ask about third-person limited versus third-person omniscient.

I nearly sank under the desk. There's more than one kind of third-person? I was so, so screwed.

Ten years later, the point of view decision has turned out to be my particular nemesis. Some writers gravitate naturally to first-person. Others have never written in anything but third-person. I'm going to pretend that fiction in the second person doesn't exist. Some authors write chapters that alternate between the first and third person.

First person is the easiest POV for me. Apparently, this is fairly common when you're new to writing fiction. It feels more natural. You get to stay inside your main character's head and envision the story through that one set of eyes. When writing my first novel *Three*

Souls, it never occurred to me to use any other point of view. It just happened. The main character (MC) was rather immature and self-centred, and it was her story, so, of course, first-person. Her life was constrained to family and home, walled in by courtyards. Also, she had died recently, and it seemed more interesting to explore the quirks of the afterlife through her eyes.

My second novel *Dragon Springs Road* was also written in first-person. I wanted the story to follow a Eurasian girl's coming of age in early-twentieth-century Shanghai, where she was rejected by both Chinese and Western society. First-person allowed the reader to see and hear the racism she experienced, to feel her frustration and hurt at knowing she would never belong.

With a first-person narrator, the reader only knows as much as the main character shares, so as you plot, you need to consider ways to explain how your character learns about situations that take place "off stage." Did she discover a friend's duplicity via eavesdropping or by walking in on a scene of betrayal? Or perhaps it's when a gossipy neighbour drops the bombshell? For me, it's simpler to deliver a story in first-person.

When you're writing in third-person, you need to decide not only whether your MC will learn the awful truth via eavesdropping, a scene of betrayal, or gossipy neighbour, but also *when* the reader and the MC should find out, because the two need not happen at the same time. Sometimes, if the reader knows about this betrayal before the MC does, it builds tension as the MC stumbles around for a few more chapters, unaware of danger and heartbreak. With a third-person narrative, the story is no longer limited to what the MC perceives. The antagonist(s), love interest, and supporting characters get to have their say. As the story unfolds, you have more options for telling about the who, when, why, and where. And that means more decisions about the storylines to sort through: how to structure POV, timeline, and scenes to achieve maximum impact.

When it came to *The Library of Legends*, I reluctantly left the comfort zone and switched to a third-person narrative. The decision had everything to do with scope. I did start out writing in first-person, but it became clear very quickly that a single first-person POV was inadequate to inform readers of the complexities of that era. The historical background was so epic and layered with political and social turmoil, class differences, and traditional Chinese versus Western thinking.

The novel really had only one MC, but the use of third-party POV allowed the narrative to shift. Sometimes it was third-person limited — which is like putting the camera right in your character's face to catch all their inner thoughts. Sometimes it was third-person omniscient — which allows you to draw back with that camera and offer insights or information your characters couldn't possibly bring to the story in a plausible manner.

The Library of Legends centres around university students who become refugees in their own country. Third-person limited was most effective when conveying their responses to new experiences, such as the shock of seeing rural poverty. But, in order to build a sense of place, third-person omniscient was more flexible, providing a broader brush to paint the historical and political landscape, as well as comment on the social changes rolling through China. I felt I could do this less intrusively than trying to force a lot of background information into dialogue or thoughts.

My current work-in-progress features two main characters: two women from very different cultures whose lives collide. Originally I wanted to stick with a single POV, but my agent suggested I try the dual-narrator approach since the women are so different. And, of course, there was the POV decision. Both in first-person, or both in third-person? Maybe one in each? I must admit my first ten thousand words were in first-person, alternating between the two women. But again, first-person wouldn't support the story structure needed to deliver all the elements I wanted in the novel. After asking around and getting assurance from other authors, I settled on third-person for both characters.

It hasn't been easy writing dual narratives. It's meant new challenges. I have to make sure each character gets an equal share of the storytelling, that each woman's story arc is as compelling as the other's while keeping the pace moving for both. Hardest of all has been deciding which one of them should own the narrative when their stories intersect — or shift to third-person omniscient.

There are days when I just plod along with grim determination and drive for word count. Most days, actually. Reminding myself that an ugly first draft is just the first stage in getting the story down, nose to tail, and that the revision stage is where I can improve the writing. Much as I whine, with each book comes an opportunity to improve writing skills. I suspect POV will always be a tough one for me, that third-person will never feel as natural as first-person. But as practitioners of the craft, we can't hide within our comfort zones. We must recognize that comfort zones can also be weaknesses that limit our ability to tell a story. We must work through them to acquire the toolbox we need.

PROMPT:

Pick a chapter from a favourite book or a work-in-progress that involves more than one character. Rewrite it using a different POV. If in third-person, change to first and vice versa. Notice whether this makes you see the story differently, whether there are things a character can no longer comment upon or observations that are no longer valid. Does this perspective allow you to build a sense of place, provide a broader brush to paint the historical and political landscape, as well as comment on the social changes of the era? Similarly, does this POV give you more of the character's thoughts, motivations, and individual needs? Perhaps, as a result of POV change, the narrative is able to provide more or fewer insights into character and motivation.

CHARACTER CREATES PLOT

CAROLINE ADDERSON

"I'm terrible at plotting!"

Despite all the writing manuals and instructional blogs on the subject, this is one of the commonest complaints heard in creative writing classrooms. A quick search on the Vancouver Public Library's website offers, to name but a few: *Mastering Plot Twists: How to Use Suspense, Targeted Storytelling Strategies, and Structure to Captivate Your Readers; Building Fiction: How to Develop Plot and Structure; Writing the Novel: From Plot to Print; Writing Blockbuster Plots: A Step-by-Step Guide to Mastering Plot, Structure, and Scene;* and *Plot: How to build short stories and novels that don't sag, fizzle, or trail off in scraps of frustrated revision — and how to rescue stories that do.* All of them promise to demystify the initial incident, rising action, climax, and denouement. There are only four steps! So why is this so hard?

I think that plotting is difficult for many writers because, by definition, it is assumed to be a conscious and mechanical process when, in fact, intuition plays a huge role. The Oxford English Dictionary defines plot as, "The plan or scheme of a literary work; the interrelationship of the main events in a play, novel, film, etc." Plans and schemes, like bank heists, are usually worked out ahead of time, but this doesn't necessarily happen when you are writing a story or novel. The writer might start with a blank screen or only an image or two. Even those who construct a fully developed plot line before writing are often forced to abandon it as soon as the story gets going. Furthermore, if you think of a narrative solely in terms of plot, an essential story element is left out: character.

Stories are about people — the things they do, what happens to them, how they think and feel about these events, and, most importantly, how they change as a result. Even if you are writing in a genre where a preconceived plot would be advisable (the five-volume fantasy series, for example, or the nine hundred-page intergenerational saga), you must create characters who will convincingly take part in the story's events.

On the page, character is revealed to the reader through a complex interplay of description (by the narrator and by other characters), contrasting characters (foils), thoughts, action, dialogue, body language, gesture, and symbolic association. Even the character's name suggests something about them. These are details that writers invent for their characters before *and* during the writing process, and they will obviously affect the plot. However, the character element that is most connected to plot, which in fact *creates* the plot, is motivation. What does the character want? What the character wants is reflected in how the character acts. With regard to the protagonist of the story, these actions become the drama of the plotline.

How this works in practice can be illustrated in a simple exercise. Here are three possible motivations: love, revenge, adventure. Let's apply these motivations to the same imaginary situation: a woman (let's call her Amy) comes home from a weekend business trip and finds that her partner has packed up and left.

If Amy's motivation is love, and if Amy loves her partner, she will have an emotional reaction — shock at first. Once the shock subsides, she'll act according to her motivation. Since she loves her partner, she'll want to make sure she or he is safe. If contacting their mutual friends about the disappearance gives her no answers, she'll likely call the police. Every step she takes to find her partner will be based on her motivation: love. She loves her partner; her partner loves her. Therefore, they must be reunited. If, during the story, Amy discovers that her partner has actually left her for someone else, then Amy's story will become about regaining their love or finding love somewhere else. This could happen early or late in the story, which would affect its plot. Ultimately, everything that happens in the story, everything that Amy *makes happen*, must be centred around her desire for love.

If Amy's motivation is revenge, the story will be entirely different. Say Amy is already nursing grievances about the relationship. When she comes home and finds her partner missing, her shock will dissipate much faster than in the previous version. Likely, it will turn to rage, rage at the deception and how she has wasted part of her life on an unworthy person. Then she will begin to scheme her revenge for this betrayal. The first person she'll likely call is her lawyer.

But if Amy's motivation is adventure, the story will be different again. After the initial shock, Amy may realize that this is an opportunity for her to make a change in her life. She's probably felt stifled for ages in that suburban townhouse! Maybe she decides to sell everything and travel the world or sign up to volunteer abroad. *This* Amy will phone her real estate agent.

This example is simple in the extreme, but it does serve to show the intimate connection between motivation and plot. Character motivation is usually much more nuanced and layered. For example, if a character wants money, it's useful to ask why. Does money imply success? Who does he want to impress? His parents? Why? Did he feel unloved as a child? If so, perhaps the story is actually about someone with so deep a desire for unconditional love that he doesn't even recognize the true source of his relentless pursuit of financial gain. Unlike in real life, where most people have multiple motivations, even conflicting ones (for example: I want to be a writer *and* I want to earn a lot of money), characters have one consistent motivation throughout the story or novel. They may be blind to their own true motivation — as indeed their creators may be for several drafts — but it is nevertheless the little engine making the narrative run. When writers lament that they don't know how to plot or they don't know what happens next in the story, it is usually not the result of a plot problem but a character problem.

But how can you tell what your protagonist wants? This is where intuition comes into play. The writer must think deeply about her character. She must come to understand so much more about this imaginary person than is ever revealed on the page so that the protagonist becomes the person closest to the writer. Your characters *are*, in fact, the closest people to you because they live inside you, gestated in your imagination. Eventually, if you put the effort in, first consciously then subconsciously (this best friend of the writer usually takes on the heavy lifting at a certain point), you will feel the yearnings of your character as clearly as you feel your own. At this point, your protagonist will take charge of your imagination and simply show you what must happen next. Only part of this process is planned. Much of it happens in little bursts of insight, usually when you are not even writing (keep that notebook handy!). Some of it happens on the page as you proceed through the many drafts required to produce a publishable story or novel. The writers who are most likely to succeed are the ones who are able to find satisfaction, even joy, in this slow revelation.

PROMPT:

This is a fun exercise to help you understand the motivation of your protagonist. First, read through the obituaries in your newspaper. Choose a couple of the more engaging ones, and try to figure out what might have been the "driving force" in that person's life. (As mentioned above, real people usually have multiple motivations, so narrow in on just one. For a world traveller, it might be "adventure." For a much-married person, it might be "love.")

Next, write an obituary for the protagonist of your story or novel. This will oblige you to imagine your character far beyond the time-frame of your story, from childhood all the way to death. Is there some logic to where they started and where they ended up? What did they do with their life? What drove them? If it turns out to be external circumstances (instead of making choices: things happen *to* them), this may signal that you have a passive protagonist. (Time to reimagine!) Now apply this new understanding to your story or novel. Is this character's motivation making your novel or story tick?

ON PRAXIS

AISLINN HUNTER

As a voice-driven writer (and as a poet/novelist), I often struggle with plot. In early drafts of my prose, things happen in the narrative (a border is crossed; a man proposes drunkenly to a woman he knows will say no) but not things that are necessarily of *consequence*: events that cause further complicating events to happen. Technically, plot is the "because" part of your story or narrative: because A happens, then B occurs, because B occurs, then C, and so on. Plot is like the spine of your book this way: it's what holds a story together. It's the line of action that a character's development and change stem from.

I remember being at a loss midway through my third novel (and eighth book), *The Certainties*, as to what kind of plot point should occur next. My character — and I — were stuck. So, I asked myself the most basic question a writer can ask about their floundering character: "What does he want at this point in the narrative?" I knew the answer was to commit suicide. So, I asked, "What does he need?" and the answer was a jug for water to take the morphine pills he was carrying. And so, my character got up to go get his jug. This "want" led him to the guard who was keeping him under house arrest, a "want" which then took the two of them to the hotel kitchen to source a jug ... and on and on to a whole series of actions and reactions.

What I loved about the jug solution was that it represented a small want. Plot points, especially the subtle ones, can be seemingly innocuous (even to the writer during a first draft). Much like those mechanisms we rely on in our own daily lives — the must-dos and desires that get us up and out of bed — a plot point is a want *that turns into action*; in my case, a want that turns a character away from his balcony by the sea and toward a series of catastrophes.

"Praxis" — which comes to literary theory largely through Aristotle's *Poetics* — is usually understood as "action" or "doing." As a concept, it's been subject to different interpretations over the centuries. Aristotle seems to have equated the word with an external force, paring off the action undertaken by a character ("praxis") from the moral state of the character ("ethos") and the feelings or passions that lead the character to action ("pathos"). But critics working over the last century have tended to fold the idea of a character's feelings or motivation in the drama (their "pathos") into the concept of praxis. This seems apt to me, for even when our motivations are largely mysterious, they're still tied intrinsically and palpably to why we do what we do.

To illustrate this a bit more concretely, let's go back to the jug. The *action* my protagonist takes is to ask the guard for a jug to wash with, as there isn't a jug in his room. This is an action, but the action is married to *why* he asks for a jug and the why list would be a long one: he's a refugee trapped in a difficult situation with no realistic way out, he's exhausted by war, he's ill, he's worried he's endangering his friends who are younger and stronger, he's lived a good life; all of that but also, more practically, he doesn't want to be caught by his friends on his way to and from the bathroom with his pills, and he has standards for himself: he doesn't want to take his morphine tablets in a dirty shared bathroom, and he wants the dignity of his bed. I call these impulses (*why* he wants a jug) "praxis" — intentions that are embedded within his actions, which are, therefore, important support structures to a work's plot. Dante had a phrase for this form of motivated action — he called it "movement of spirit," and I think of praxis like that: the internal (and often unwritten but implied) state of a character that leads to (and is, therefore, a part of) each action they take.

Praxis — in the old-fashioned sense of plain doing, of action — untainted by a psyche's desire, doesn't seem to suit contemporary fiction. I teach a lot of first-year creative writing classes, and every semester, one student inevitably writes a story about a psychopath: a character who does bad things (often randomly and to strangers) with no reason, with no inner praxis. An individual who, machine-like, is devoid of any complex "why" dynamics. Events might occur in this story, but often they're unrelated and unmotivated incidents. (Murder isn't a plot point unless it causes further events to happen; until it does, it's just an "incident" and of little consequence to our story, even if alarming.) In workshops of these stories, the key theme that emerges is that the readers of the story don't care about what they're reading. They feel like they're being led around a senseless world, being shown a series of events that cause alarm but have no rationale. The *doing* isn't enough for them; they want to know *why*.

Aristotle was alive at a time when events large and small could be attributed to gods who, bored on weekends, might roll their proverbial dice above the heads of the citizens below. Actions and events weren't always as readily attributed to human agency as actions and events are now. In the twenty-first century, action is rarely pared away from motivation. What does this mean for us writers? Well, action without intention leads to flat reading. Action with too much intention feels clumsy and telling. This can be resolved by balancing characterization and backstory or flashbacks with forward-action, by a mature handling of time. We need to give readers a palpable sense of a historied life, a life rife with informing instances, but this informing information needs to sit in balance with a plot-driven story rich in forward action. If we are to believe my protagonist wouldn't deign to take his morphine in a dingy shared bathroom, we need to see in other parts of the book the lifestyle to which he was accustomed. We need to see his manners and sense of decorum and also, maybe, to sense the idea that he is looking for a small excuse to defer his suicide because he is still so very much in love with the world.

Ultimately, the tricky thing about praxis (in its motivation-plus-action model) is that while it's a vital aspect of a narrative, it's usually best left implied. The whole of a book's characterisation goes into building praxis. In this way, it's like a colour or texture (an electric impulse) that rides under every sentence and line in a work of literary art. At its best, it often goes half-articulated — rarely stated. Because to state the "why" of an individual's actions is to reduce that action to one overblown thing, when the "why" of human existence and human action and reaction is largely mysterious, even to the actors.

In poetry workshops, whether my students and I are working on narrative or lyric poems, we talk about praxis too: *why* did the poet or persona bring this poem (event) into being? What do we sense was the underlying motivation for the poem: what crisis, question, concern led to this utterance. These textures, or wellsprings, should always be palpable in a great work of art (though again, often unsaid or unequated) because art is borne from urgency and not boredom, from concerns that are multi-faceted and not trivial. If the author, narrator, or characters are acting out of a real-seeming prompt — out of a situation that launches them into "doing" or "saying" — then we will follow them along on their journey. We will trust, as readers, that the journey matters, that it has stakes for the character or the figure in the work, and maybe (and this is the wonder of literature), also for us.

PROMPT:
Take a published story by an author you admire. Underline the main causal chain of action (the plot) in one colour (because A then B, because B then C, etc.), and underline the incidents that occur in the story (events without causality) in another colour. (One of a writer's tricks is to make sure their story has enough incidents that the plot line isn't overly transparent or expected, like the train you see coming a mile down the tracks.) Look at the balance between plot points and incidents. Then look at a story of your own and do the same. Then ask yourself how the reader might sense the motivation for your character's choices and actions. Do we know enough about this character that we can intuit some of the reasons they spring into action as they do? (They grew up in a broken home, their brother

bullied them, they lost their job, etc.) One way to strengthen your own understanding of your character is to isolate an action then ask yourself to list five reasons why your character chose that one path of action in particular when there were other options available. Then ask yourself if any of those reasons are palpable in your story and if they're palpable enough.

Good luck with your writing!

PROXIMITY IN OUR WRITING, WITH OTHER WRITERS & WITH OUR READERS

BETSY WARLAND

Over the past five decades, I have been on a quest to understand the key role proximity plays in my own writing: when I teach and mentor other writers, when I edit other writers' manuscripts, and in my companionship with writers and authors.

The etymology of *proximity* goes back to: *"nearness, closeness."*

Evoking the narrative's nearness is what every piece of compelling writing has in common — it draws the reader deeply in — regardless of genre. The arduous quest of how to do this with every piece of writing makes our companionship with other writers all the more crucial. Why? Non-literary writers explain and elaborate. Literary writers evoke. These are profoundly different approaches to writing. As literary writers, we must learn precisely how to do this with every narrative we write.

My quest for understanding proximity began in Toronto in the early 1970s. At that time, creative writing courses and workshops were taught by male writers who maintained that subject matters based on the lived experiences of women were not literary topics. Although I was learning the essential skills of craft, feedback on my subjects and point of view was dismissive.

So, I approached the Toronto YWCA with the idea of offering a women writers' workshop. I wondered: "Would there be enough registrants to even run it?"

One hundred and fifty women writers registered!

Within a year, we formed the Toronto Women's Writing Collective that produced workshops, readings, anthologies, a literary journal, and public literary events. The critical feedback and companionship in those workshops and numerous public readings enabled me to test out my topics and trust what kind of proximities each poem required. Did the poem's content keep the reader close up throughout? Or did it hold the reader in the middle distance? Or did it keep the reader in panorama proximity throughout? Or did the poem's content track and evoke a shifting proximity? All these factors enabled me to finish my manuscript, and my first book was published in 1981.

I then moved to Vancouver. I began teaching creative writing, and five books later, in 1999, I was asked to design a Simon Fraser University Continuing Studies non-credit creative writing certificate program. The Writers Studio (TWS) created new accessibility and, in turn, proximity, based "on learning in community," and it attracted a much broader range of writers seeking professional training. This dynamic diversity is evident in TWS alumni books that have significantly enriched Canadian literature.

The acts of thinking, imagining, writing, revising, reading, training in creative writing, and finding companionship are interdependent acts of proximity, like the fascia that holds our organs, blood vessels, bones, nerve fibers, and muscles together.

Writing this essay is an example.

From the early drafts to submitting a solid but not resolved draft to the editors twice, to receiving their feedback and thinking over their comments, to, subsequently, my numerous sessions of revisions — each time noticing aspects I'd skimmed over, left out, or were non sequiturs — this process has been an exercise in fine-tuning proximity. When all aspects of proximity are accurately activated, the narrative lifts off the page effortlessly.

A common proximity error is for the writer to do the heavy lifting for our reader. One example is frequent summation (instead of evoking via scenes, dialogue, atmosphere, extended metaphor, etc.). Another error is billboarding (inserting a cue explaining what a poem, scene, or chapter means). Common, as well, is our numbing the reader by writing the narrative at the same pace throughout, regardless of what is transpiring. This tendency can be okay when we're just getting a first draft down, but then, in subsequent drafts, we must evoke ("score" as in musical notation) the proximity accurately. When we fail to do so, the narrative is oddly flat: monotone.

Another crucial reason to pay attention to creating shifting proximities is our tendency to leave out the narrative's switchbacks — the zigzag storytelling trajectory of a character or a personal account — that inherently transpire regardless of genre.

Switchbacks are crucial. Essential.

Why? They embody lived experience. All forms of perception build incrementally — transpire consciously and subconsciously — over a length of time. It's a process of absorbing/abandoning/reabsorbing. Our own switchbacks, as well as our characters', are partial, puzzling, false, exciting, frightening, enlightening, misunderstood, creative, comforting, and, sometimes, subject to untenable grandiosity!

They are the body language of every vibrant and engrossing narrative.

Regardless of genre and length, every narrative we write is like climbing a mountain that we must zigzag countless times in order to get to the top. Some switchbacks reveal an entirely new view, others reveal a similar view from a different perspective, and some are dead ends. The narrative builds incrementally. Unforeseeably.

All forms of emotional, intellectual, physical, spiritual, and sociopolitical awareness manifest in switchbacks, loops, reversals, and returns. When we fail to evoke this process accurately, we keep the reader emotionally, intellectually, and viscerally on the outside of the narrative. There is a lack of authenticity. Discovery. Our readers remain dispassionate observers robbed of the sensations of deduction that accumulatively enable them to gain their own insights; access their own feelings.

Every narrative we write knows precisely what it is and is not about, what its inherent form is (and is not), and most crucially, how to deeply engage its reader.

When there are problems in a manuscript or piece of writing, they are almost always proximity problems. A piece of writing that embodies searching and accumulating revelation (large and small) is a piece of writing that deeply engages us. Why? It's authentic. Visceral. True to lived experience. My prompt below provides one strategy for how to identify and explore proximity problems.

My 2000 memoir, *Bloodroot: Tracing the Untelling of Motherloss*, taught me a great deal about how crucial proximity is. It was my first book-length narrative in the form of entries of various lengths and genres. The un-inscribed spaces I scored on the page embodied what could partially be known or never be known, said, or understood. When aspects of the narrative could be told in a traditional manner, the space was fully occupied with standard prose. When other parts of the story were more tentative — had flashes of memory or insight — these pages were partially occupied. And there were pages that held a solitary sentence of insight or fear floating alone. This scoring gave the reader space to absorb and navigate the feelings (and their own related memories) that the difficult passages in *Bloodroot* evoked.

My agent advised me that no publisher would agree to the use of so much unconventional blank space. Consequently, I deleted the spacing, inserted asterisks between each entry, then sent the manuscript to my decades-long first readers.

Silence.

This had never happened before.

When I enquired why they reported it was hard to read, to stick with. They stalled.

I rescored it exactly as it was before with the blank spacing. No other changes were made. The outcome changed dramatically. They couldn't put it down — reported that it was the best book I had ever written. The form embodied the emotional logic of how the story actually unfolded, and it also created the pacing readers needed.

Years later, when giving readings from *Bloodroot*, I continue to include the pauses. I need the pauses. So does the audience. One of my most popular books, a 2021 second edition of *Bloodroot*, includes a new essay about what that book taught me as a writer.

As writers, whether it is in our writing practice or with other writers, proximity is bedrock. We need one another's encouragement, but we also need one another's artistic challenges and ethical observations. This companionship differs from our other companionships. I can know a writer's writing and writing life quite deeply, yet have cursory knowledge about their private life, their work life, the details of their background. It is a different kind of intimacy based considerably more on the unknown than the known, on what our dissimilarities shed light on more than our likenesses.

Whichever way you look at it, being a student of proximity is our life-long quest.

PROMPT:
Identifying Proximity Problems Structurally
This exercise is helpful in gaining insights as to where the narrative is faltering, particularly when your dissatisfaction with the narrative is nebulous. Focusing visually on the architecture or structure of the narrative — oversights, absences, tangents, redundancies, summarizing — verses evoking, can reveal where revisions are needed.

1. Select three to five poems, five short prose pieces, or five pages from a longer prose piece that you are vexed by or dissatisfied with.

2. Review these pages *visually* (don't focus on content).

3. With poetry, are most of the poetic lines and stanzas essentially the same length and structure? Are the poems all essentially the same length?

4. With prose, are the sentences, paragraphs, and sections (if applicable) essentially the same length and structure?

5. What impression (again, *only visually*) do you get? For example, if almost all the paragraphs or stanzas (excepting closed poetic forms) are the same length, what sensation or impression does that evoke in you?

6. Now look at the content and let it guide you to where you need to make changes that embody each line/sentence and paragraph/stanza more accurately, powerfully, evocatively. Mark or highlight these areas.

7. Now, refine your evaluation even more and study how each line or sentence opens and closes for repetition and dulling effect, such as starting a line or sentence in the same way ("The..." or "I...," etc.).

8. Then, identify over-used words or phrases and replace them with other vocabulary that is more evocative and specific to their content.

9. Finally, rewrite the spots or areas you have summarized or explained that need to bring the reader closer via dialogue, extended metaphor, deeper reflection, expanding a pivotal scene, or telling detail.

Create a new draft based on these revisions and see what you find out.

You can access additional thoughts in my book *Breathing the Page: Reading the Act of Writing*. A sample chapter on proximity can be found on betsywarland.com.

THE RUPTURE

WAYDE COMPTON

For years now, I have used a piece of metathinking, as a writer and instructor, that can, unlike most aspects of creative writing, be shown in a graph. I call it "the rupture." It represents an experience I noticed a long time ago in my own work, but that, I think, is common to all writers. I've seen the effect of the rupture with students, I've noted when it has happened in my own projects, and I have heard other writers talk about it, each in their own words, using different terms. You could surely describe it many different ways. But I suspect the experience itself is pretty close to universal.

The graph is as simple as can be and what it depicts is the plan and execution of any single piece of writing, whether it is a short lyric poem, a story, a novel, an essay, or a memoir. Any single piece of writing really. It's a simple line with two ends and an X in the middle:

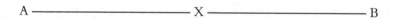

A ———————————————— X ———————————————— B

The reason why this is "metathinking" (thinking about *how* you think) is that the graph does not represent something formal, like a plot structure or theme, in a piece of writing. What the line represents is a writer's plan to write something. A is where the idea forms. B is where the writer imagines the project will end. The line is the time spent drafting. (We'll get to what the X is soon.)

What kind of person is a writer when they are at the A, the beginning, when they are imagining writing a poem, essay, story, or anything? I think at this point in the process you ought to be courageous and brave. Ambitious. You've decided you might be able to write one of those things and that it will be good enough for someone else to read. You need some vision at this point, even a bit of arrogance, to be honest. You're embarking on something, and, to do that, you need at least some provisional faith in this big dream.

How about over there at the B? Well, that is in the imagined future. That's where you figure your project will be completed, when it becomes a finished poem, essay, novel. Who is the writer at that point? Satisfied that the job is done, you suppose, but you're not there yet. It is in the hazy future.

So, the line is how you expect things will go when you set out to write, and it's why you can say to yourself, "I'm working on a novel (or memoir, or play, or whatever)."

And here is where the X comes in.

The X is this experience I call "the rupture." It's the point at which your original plan, your idea of what it is you're writing, falls apart. I put it in the middle in the graph above, but it can be anywhere. Near the start, near the end. Also, it can be something you write up to, as in you actually start drafting, and it happens during the process. Or you can write past it. You might complete the whole project because you blew past the rupture, either denying it or failing to notice it.

Wherever it shows up, the rupture is the point at which your original vision for this project, the one you were ambitious and maybe even arrogant about (productively so) at the start, fails. How does it fail? It's usually hard to perceive why or how it's failing when it happens, but you know it is. The thing you meant to do is not working; something seems to be missing; it all just feels off; it is not as you expected; it is not matching your ambitions. This can be something you notice or something that is pointed out to you. But it is the point where you realize your original vision just isn't flying.

And it's a bad feeling. A terrible one. It's easy to ignore it and carry on, which is how unpublishable things often get finished. And if you accept it, it's easy for it to paralyze you and make you stop writing because failures feel debilitating. But the point of this essay, and the reason this is "metathinking," is that what you're at war with when the rupture happens is your pretence and, in a real sense, your fears. Because the rupture, as awful as it feels, is usually the assertion of great opportunity. What feels like the failure of a project is, in disguise, the chance to make it better, if you're willing to adapt and listen.

Here's why: when we set out to write something, at point A, we are often playing it safer than we realize we are. Our ambitions match our opinions and personal idiosyncrasies, our pretences, and our pet topics. The things we know well and feel relatively comfortable taking on. Those are fine, to start with, because they get us writing. But they're also often as flat on the page as they are safe. Because they are safe and well-trod, they aren't necessarily where the real insight is, the breakthrough moments that literature can give the *author*, not just the reader.

An example from my own writing life: my first book of poems, *49th Parallel Psalm*, is about the arrival of the first Black population to British Columbia in the nineteenth century. I wrote it to explore my own cultural position as a person of African descent in BC, where our history is little known or talked about. At point A, my ambition was to write this history in a way that might have made me feel strong and grounded, had it existed when I was younger. The rupture point of the early draft came when I realized the heroic account of the Black pioneers I was writing was ringing false. I had thought what I wanted was an epic of heroism, but what was peeking out through the manuscript was more uncertain, more about the ambivalence of identity. Rather than an epic, the quiet question "why does this matter to me?" kept appearing in my poems. This was not the book I had meant to write, and I wasn't even sure I liked it. So, I stopped writing for months.

That was the rupture.

But here is how it's more than a failure, but rather is also an opportunity. Because I gradually realized that the heroic concept I had started with was simply not as interesting or as honest as what was trying to get through, that identity is fragile, and that my *need* for Black heroes was more interesting than trying to make ordinary historical figures into heroes. You can see how this is a difficult realization, a less comfortable and more vulnerable direction. But I gradually came to see that this rupture of the original idea had produced a much more mature theme. So, I accepted the failure of the original vision and wrote into that rupture to completion. The book remains in print and feels, in some ways, bigger than my own thinking at the time. The writing of it taught me something and was not a delivery system for my opinions. That is all due to this rupture effect and letting it show the way during the process.

As a teacher, I saw student writers go through similar processes on their way to publication. I later wondered if this rupture always happens. For me, it does. And here is the use of recognising it: while ruptures always feel bad — there's really no way around that; they feel traumatic because they are the death of your first hopes — they are nevertheless gifts. Sometimes they are thematic and sometimes formal. For one of my books, the rupture came when I realised I was writing it in the wrong narrative mode, and the revision, I guessed, would take a year. That's traumatic, sure. But I've come to also think of that as merely part of the writing process. And even, perhaps, the most important part of the process. It feels bad at first, but it doesn't paralyze me for months anymore. Maybe a few days while I get used to the unexpected idea that has emerged. I reflect and reorient fairly quickly now and accept it as necessary. I think of the rupture as the way an idea you are not quite ready for at the start can find its way through, nevertheless. And like it or not, it's usually the better idea because it's the one that arrives out of the writing itself.

So, after you accept the rupture and write into it, which can be harrowing, you're a different kind of writer now. If at point A you were ambitious, after the rupture, you will find that you must move toward point B with humility. You're serving a story or poem or essay that's a little bigger than you now, that's a little beyond your favoured image of yourself, as a writer or a person, and out there in the territory of things that are challenging, sometimes greatly so, which is also the source of their power. If you find yourself completing a project after such a point and feel like it's telling you how it has to be written, then it's likely you're serving that rupture well.

And this is why it's nothing to fear. I look forward to that moment of fracture now. I give myself a day or two to feel bad about it. I readjust. I rethink. And I get to work uncovering what the writing says it needs to be.

PROMPT:

After reviewing my theory of the rupture, consider one of your recent writing projects. One that you have been unable to finish or have completed in a way that is not satisfactory to you. Try to identify a rupture moment within it. What was your intention for the project at the start? Where did the project founder or stray from your original intentions for it? What challenging ideas were revealed in that moment? Write these down as a way of practising rupture-oriented metathinking and consider how this moment of deviation from the original idea may actually point the way forward to a wholly new direction.

SYNECDOCHE – REWRITING A NOVEL: HOW TO HOLD THE WHOLE IN MIND, WHILE REWRITING THE PART

CLAUDIA CASPER

While first impressions, in their partialness, can mislead — a shy person can read as arrogant, an insecure person as confident — the flood of provisional, contextual information we process in one-tenth of a second to seven seconds when we first meet someone is mind-blowing. If the connection continues, the long process of refining what we think we know about someone from that first impression — their strength, health, personality, mood, threat, alliance, class, style, age, gender, culture, etc. — goes on forever.

Readers' brains do something similar when they pick up a book and read the first few pages. They're encountering something new, decoding a fresh context, a new set of rules, forming an impression. Their brains start tracking for unanswered questions, inconsistencies, conflict, trajectories of meaning.

Writing a novel and rewriting it, however, is a completely different process. It requires holding the whole book in your consciousness in some way that is quasi-simultaneous while you work on a part. How is this possible? Our brains, through language, can perform another magical feat called synecdoche, a rhetorical term derived from the Greek word meaning "simultaneous meaning," where the part is made to stand for the whole or vice versa. Everyday examples of synecdoche are terms like "green thumb" standing for a gifted gardener, "twinkle toes" for a great dancer, or "sharp threads" for a great piece of clothing. Rewriting a first draft requires this mental ability.

There are two basic approaches to rewriting, with every variation in between. In one, the writer knows the structure of their novel right from the start. Carol Shields, for example, would structure her novels around a period of time in her protagonist's life. She referred to her structure as the hanger on which she hung her story. Her discipline was to write two pages a day, then, the following day, rewrite those two pages until she was satisfied, then write the next two. By the time she was finished, no doubt with some retracing of steps along the way, she had a final draft that needed very few revisions.

I wish I had this process. It's time-efficient, brain-efficient, organized, and, I imagine, less stressful than my own, which lies at the other end of the spectrum. I write a first draft to discover what my novel is. Eden Robinson calls this the vomit draft. The most depressing stage in my writing process is rereading this first draft. Instant two-week depression. I rediscover how thoroughly lead is not gold. So much of this version is scaffolding, as Betsy Warland calls it, writing that is me thinking on paper to myself; so many words and scenes are flat and superfluous to a reader. Somewhere near the end of that two-week depression, however, my mind starts to quicken. My inner alchemist reanimates. The shape of what my novel needs to become starts revealing itself. I'm back in the saddle (this is *so* a metaphor since, in reality, horses know the instant I mount that I'm not the boss and head for the barn). For me, the second draft is the real substantive writing of the novel. The first draft is wildly generative; the second draft is when the house gets built. (Note the free rein [sic] I'm giving myself to mix metaphors. Don't try this at home.)

Rereading my first draft, in fact, rereading any draft of a novel, requires a prodigious amount of memory. I think of it as repacking the novel into my brain, as if my mind were a suitcase. Once done, I can begin to see what the draft is, intuit its shape as a whole, its weight, its voice, its movement. I can begin the brain-aching process of reordering the story, making the narrative structure intentional, bringing out themes, paying attention to the nuances of the experiential journey I want to take my reader on, and, at the same time, deepening my characters, understanding their motivation and behaviour.

Confession: if I'm intrigued by the structure of a novel I am reading, I will skip to the end and read it first so I can see how the author is building their story.

Once the first draft is repacked into my memory, I start making diagrams. Every author's brain is unique and, thus, the way they visualize their story is going to be unique. What you are looking for at this stage is a way for the part to stand for the whole, a true mnemonic that triggers enough of your memory that you understand what you are moving or shaping.

For my first two novels, I used a white Bristol board and wrote the key elements — themes, events, and ideas — floating in space. Then I drew lines of connection between them, creating a loose spiderweb with short notes to myself, attached where needed. After a solid second draft was completed, I printed the novel out and attached colour-coded Post-it Notes to identify themes and plots, so I could see how they were paced and in what order.

For my third novel, I went to an art supply store (a heavenly place for novelists looking for ways to schematize their work) and bought a long oblong sketchbook (8" x 24.5") and coloured highlighters. I drew two long straight lines, one above the other. The top line represented the chronological sequence of events, and the bottom line represented the narrative order of revelation. I colour-coded each entry with a highlighter specific to a character or narrative thread. Underneath the narrative line, I noted the number of pages of each entry, beat, or chapter to get a sense of the rhythm and music of the novel.[1]

Many writers use software like Scrivener or Microsoft Excel to map out the structure of their novels. They are able to hold multiple screens or files in mind without actually seeing them and can toggle back and forth following their thought processes. My brain does not have that abstract gymnastic ability.

Neurological studies[2] have shown that we use different parts of our brain when we read an e-book versus a physical book, when we write using paper and pen versus fingers pressing keys to make images appear on a screen. I experience the computer screen as an extension of my mind. So, for me to be able to analyze my novel as a whole, I need to place it outside my mind to some extent; I need a physical diagram. Only then can I move parts around, whether that means deleting or adding a scene, removing or adding a character, changing the order of revelation. Only then can I visualize how each change will affect the narrative flow and the story as a whole.

Whatever shape your diagram takes, whatever synecdochic elements you use to rearrange the parts of the whole, no schema can replace the actual experience of reading a novel from the beginning to the end, of going on the journey, as much as you can, with the reader and intuiting what they might experience word by word, sentence by sentence, scene by scene. Just as no one can fully control the information someone absorbs in a first impression, no author can fully control the experience your reader has reading your novel. Story will always resist domestication, and that's a good thing.

1. An author's conception of what blocks make up their story is going to differ. For some, it will be scenes; for others, beats that move the plot forward; for others, it will be chapters.

2. There have been many important studies on this over the years, but this article in *Scientific American* is particularly interesting: scientificamerican.com/article/reading-paper-screens/

PROMPT:
Using a large surface (Bristol board, large sheet of paper, extra-long sheet of paper), preferably with different colour pens or highlighters, map out the structure of your novel. See what your mind wants to create. Do you want a satellite visual of your piece or a linear one? Maybe try both and note the difference in how each works for you to understand your work as a whole while seeing the pieces it is made of.

Draw two lines. On the top, place the chronological order of events. On the bottom, place the narrative order of events. Are they the same?

What happens if you alter the narrative order? In my experience, a change in narrative order can also significantly change the meaning of the whole work, the effect on the reader, even the genre (who done it, for example, versus why done it).

Try a straight line with classic story structure demarcated: beginning; inciting incident; middle — development; mid-point; turning points; climax; end — denouement. See how your piece both fits this structure and varies from it. Reflect on what you think about the differences. Are they intentional? Do they stir up new possibilities? Do they make it more alive, interesting, creative?

TO UNPACK OR NOT TO UNPACK – THAT IS THE QUESTION

STELLA HARVEY

Writing is easy. All you have to do is cross out the wrong words.
— Mark Twain

In looking at the written work of others, I have a tendency, by way of critique, to zero in on two things: consistency of storyline and the experience I have within the story. In other words, for me, a story needs to hang together, and I want to be fully immersed in it as though I'm an invisible witness seeing, and more importantly, feeling every nuance and complication as it unfolds.

I belong to a critique group. Every writer should be so lucky. We meet monthly and review the stories of three members during our meetings. The last time I had my work critiqued, the feedback I received could be summarized in one sentence: *unpack this exposition and/or back-story into a scene.*

Funny (and I don't mean, ha, ha) how we see in the work of others the challenges we ourselves face in our own early drafts. But that's a topic for another time.

My group was absolutely right. It's not easy for a writer to see these things in the first, second, or even third draft. In these early drafts, you're telling yourself the story. You don't know the world you're creating yet or any of the details of your characters' motivation and journey. The first draft is your discovery draft, the place where you're trying to make sense of what is happening in the story.

During each iteration of the story I am writing, I ask myself: what is it I'm trying to say; what is it I'm seeing, feeling? And the answers come the more I write, the more I walk away, the more I rethink, the more I step back into the story, and, of course, the more I rewrite. It's a painful process that I absolutely hate (doesn't this sound appealing?), but I've come to learn it's the only way.

Let's go back to Mark Twain's quote. Being the compulsive editor that I am, I'd suggest a couple of additions: *Insert scenes. And not only figure out what to cross out but also what to insert.* This is what we writers face as we build a story.

All stories begin with exposition. This is how the reader is introduced to the characters, the setting, and the timeframe of the story. The writer is leading the reader forward, describing the environment we're about to enter, the people we are going to meet.

In Richard Wagamese's final and, unfortunately, unfinished novel, *Starlight,* the first chapter begins:

Emmy and the girl watched the road. It was full dark. Mosquitoes whined around their faces and they brushed them off, never taking their eyes from the gravel driveway eked out of the purple darkness like a stain. They counted the cars as they turned out and onto the main gravel road to town. Twelve of them. They waited.

With this beginning, we know it is dark, there are two characters, they are out of town, perhaps hiding.

As readers, we have further questions: who are these people, and why are they hiding?

The story continues:

Alert to any sound or movement that would send them back into the shelter of the trees. There was nothing.
"Reckon he's asleep?" the girl asked.

"You hush," she said.
The girl looked wide-eyed, the gleam of them like quicksilver in the murk. She
nodded. The man was a deerstalker. He would awake at the push of a faint
breath. Except when he was drunk as he would be now but she knew better
than to believe in the absolute deadness of drink.

With this passage, we enter a scene. We hear the characters speaking. We feel the tension between them. We understand what Emmy is worried about. We know Emmy and the girl are trying to run away before the man wakes up. We can feel their fear in our chest.

These sensory details bring the reader into the story in a way summarized bits of information simply can't.

In story, there is a place for both exposition (the telling) and, what I'll call, scenes (the showing). How do you determine when to use one versus the other? That's the question. It's not easily answered. Again, I don't think a first draft has a perfect balance of these two elements. You have to understand the story first to see where you might add scenes, those visceral bits you want your reader to experience.

So first, I'd suggest rereading your sections of exposition and ask yourself one question: am I simply summarizing information here? Why am I doing that? What is it I'm trying to avoid? Why? Is there something important here that will help me understand the character and the story? What is it, and how will it help the reader see and feel what is going on? Is this an area where I can build tension or reveal more about the character and the story? Am I telling the reader what my character is feeling, or am I showing it in a way that the reader would feel what the character is feeling? Is this a place to unpack the story? And if I do, how will it move the story along?

Okay. I know. That is definitely more than one question.

Another technique I use is to close my eyes and picture what I'm seeing from the description laid out in the exposition. I imagine I'm behind the lens of a camera. I sharpen the focus, come closer. What is going on? Who is saying what to whom? How are they sitting? Standing? What are they thinking? Once I understand what is happening, I rewrite the exposition, unpacking it into a scene with as much sensory detail as I can manage. I may not use all the details, but in drafting and redrafting, I know I will discover the specifics that need to stay and those that will be eliminated.

Here is an example of a paragraph I had written in my newest project. The setting is a dystopian world centred on walls that divide one group of people from another. Just so you know, I don't call what I'm working on *a manuscript*, let alone *a novel* until I have a first draft:

He kept his eyes open, and whenever he could, he used his skilled hands. Serving a purpose beyond his medical practice, they could snatch things. The medicines good for those on the other side were also good for his own. And if his government couldn't figure this out and do something to get what people needed, he could take care of it himself. He would never know if and when his government or those on the other side caught on until it was too late, and they dragged him off.

The feedback from my critique group regarding this paragraph was: take this out of exposition because it is ripe for tension in a scene.

And here's the rewrite:

He kept his eyes open, and, whenever he could, he used his skilled hands.

He remembered the patient he'd lost only a few weeks before. The man hadn't been taking his medicine for some time. Firas had found it and had asked him about it.

"I've lived long enough."

After the man died, and because there was no record of the pills the man had stored, Firas had taken the unused pills. Pharmacies kept close records of consumption in case anything was pilfered, overused, or stolen. He knew his patient would approve. Just like Kitianna, the man was curious about the other side and used to ask Firas, "What has happened to the world? Why do we have to live separated by a wall? We were neighbours once."

Firas would never know if and when his government or those on the other side caught on until it was too late, and they dragged him off.

There is more work to be done in this scene, but that will be work taken on when I have a full draft. And when it's done, I hope the reader will see what the character is doing, why he's doing it, and the consequences ahead.

As I said earlier, it is difficult to distinguish when to use exposition versus scenes in a first draft; so, my recommendation is to get the story down on the page. Having something to look at, besides the blank page, allows you to critique yourself and begin to question each passage.

And ask yourself one or any number of questions. But it's useful to start with one: What am I trying to do with this exposition, and would it be better done in a scene? As you answer this and other questions we've already talked about, you will bring your story to life, build authentic characters, and grab and hold your reader's attention to the very last word.

PROMPT:

1. Select a page or a paragraph of exposition from one of your stories/chapters. This might be a paragraph/page where you've introduced a character or an interaction between characters. If a page or paragraph doesn't immediately come to mind, think about a time when you've had feedback on your work and someone said, "you could really raise the tension here or make us feel what is going on if you unpacked this exposition." If you've had this feedback, please use that excerpt for this exercise.
2. Determine where you might change some of the exposition into a scene that shows what your character or characters are doing (how they are standing, sitting, etc.), what they are saying to one another, or what they are thinking.
3. Read both versions: the original and the rewrite.
4. List the differences between both versions. Some questions to consider when noting differences: Which version provides more insight into your characters and their motivations and fears? Did

you learn anything new about your character or the story you might not have known before? Which version helped you better understand what was going on? Which version helped you better sense and, more importantly, feel what was happening?

5. What has been gained with the rewrite? What has been lost? Does it matter to the overall story? Why or why not?

GHOSTS IN ELEVATORS: HOW TO EDIT A POEM

LAURA FARINA

When I write about writing, I usually lie a little bit. I share a technique that has been useful to me on occasion and pretend it's something I do all the time. There are no techniques I use all the time. I don't write every day. I use a notebook, but only sometimes. I have a file on my desktop called "Book," where, from time to time, I put poems I've written that I like, with the idea that the file will grow to become a manuscript. I have another file on my desktop called "Book #2," which I made one day when I hated most of the poems in "Book." It has three poems in it. These are the best poems I have ever written.

Still, poems get written and revised. How does that happen? For the past few days, I've been going back through old notebooks, old drafts to try and find a common thread. I think it's this: for me to write and edit material I'm proud of, I need to keep things loose and allow for new possibilities to present themselves as I go. On a practical level, this means having systems, tools, and techniques in place so that I can follow my impulses where they lead me. On a more abstract level, this means giving whatever is driving me to create free rein over my process.

I write a lot of lists: "Careers for Other People," "Shopping Mall Safety Procedures," "Towards a Taxonomy of Shadows." In a note-book, under the title "Things I'd Like to Be Able to Say in German,"

I wrote:

> *How much are you concerned about pushing this elevator button?*
> *Please tell me more about your gluten sensitivity.*
> *I am the mayor of this town!*

Then I edited the elevator line a few times:

> *Are you concerned about pushing this elevator button?*
> *Are you concerned about pushing the buttons in an elevator?*
> *Do you want to push the elevator button?*

For me (and I suspect for many poets), the process of writing and the process of revising are intertwined. They happen almost simultaneously. I write a line. I write another. I go back and revise the first line. I scrap the second line entirely. As I write, I'm trying to figure out the shape the poem will take. What am I trying to get at? This is an instinctive process — something I feel rather than something I know. Most of my poems sputter to life as a line that gets revised and revised until something about it sings to me.

With that line in place, it's easier to figure out how to write the rest of the poem.

I most often do this initial work in a notebook. I have lined notebooks of various sizes. I keep one in my desk at home, one in my desk at work, and another four or five in a box in my closet. A larger notebook is good for writing long lines; a small one is good for taking outside; a hardback one is good for writing in bed.

In another notebook, I played with the elevator line again:

Ghosts can push no buttons
in a way that keeps them from elevators.
We thought there would be seconds
but there weren't.

I remember where I was when I wrote these lines. I'd flown from Vancouver to Toronto to visit my sister. At the time, she lived in a very creaky house in the suburbs, which might be what made me think of ghosts. I remember writing in my notebook, sitting in the centre of the guest room bed, hoping the scratch of my pen on the paper would not wake up my niece.

There's a threshold that a poem crosses, where it goes from being a collection of words or images that I'm playing around with to a piece worth pursuing more seriously. Again, this is something I feel rather than something there are set parameters around. Some poems cross that threshold quickly. Some inch their way across, painful line by painful line. Some never get there. The exhilaration I feel when a piece crosses that threshold is the reason I keep writing. It's a thrilling moment of discovery — "Oh! That's what I think!" — laid out on the page.

I keep highlighters, sticky notes, and cue cards on hand to aid with this process. Sometimes I map out would-be poems in sticky notes on my wall (I write one stanza or one line on each sticky note). Sometimes I put key words from a piece I'm playing with on cue cards and move the cue cards around on my floor until they're in an order that resonates with me. Sometimes I highlight the parts of a piece I think are working and transcribe only those lines onto a fresh page or a blank document on my computer. Sometimes a walk is necessary.

Somewhere in this process, the poem gets typed up. Sometimes it is helpful to do this early — I find this is particularly true when I have a lot of ideas I'm trying to pare down. Sometimes the act of typing the poem — and the minor revisions that happen on the fly — is what helps the poem cross the threshold.

Once, my rheumatologist asked me to describe my pain. When I hesitated, he said, "Aren't you supposed to be a writer?"

In the waiting room after my appointment, I started writing a list poem called "Describe the nature of your pain." The elevator ghosts had clearly been on my mind because they showed up again:

The dead can push
no buttons.

In this way
they are kept
forever
from elevators.

Once a poem has crossed the threshold, I give it another read-through or two, making minor adjustments as I go. I make sure I don't have boring words at the ends of lines. I make sure I'm using punctuation consistently. I take out all but one (or two, sometimes three) em dashes. I love em dashes.

Then, while the piece is still a bit ragged around the edges, I bring it to my writing group or a writing coach (whose time I pay for) for feedback. It's best if I can muster the courage to get feedback on my poetry early in the revision process while I still feel vulnerable about it. I know that if I wait too long before showing others my work, I show up to the editorial process in search of praise rather than ready to get to work. I'm better able to engage if I arrive with aspects of the piece still undecided in my mind so that I can approach the editorial process in the spirit of collaboration.

I know I'm receiving a good edit when it makes space for my writing practice and process within the feedback; when it acknowledges that the work I am going to have to do on these revisions is mine alone and that the process of coming to the right solution is mine, too. I'm suspicious of rewrites unless they come infrequently and are so very, very good that when I receive them, they feel like gifts. The right change for my poem will be particular to my poem and will most often come from me as I think through the feedback I've received from a good editor.

"Describe the nature of your pain" became a long poem in numbered sections about how mundane chronic pain can be. I renamed it "Diagnostic Tool." When all the pieces fell into place, I sent it to my coach for an edit. He wrote, "'In this way' aren't interesting — or necessary — words." True enough.

The dead can push
no buttons.

They are kept
forever
from elevators.

Poems never feel done to me. Instead, I stop when editing starts making the poem worse. No, that's a lie. I keep editing, feel frustrated, and question whether I'm any good. Then I revert to a previous draft and feel a little better about myself.

And wait.

And wait some more.

Is there anything else the poem needs me to do?

Maybe put in an em dash. Maybe take it out again.

Maybe read the poem to a friend. Maybe not.

Maybe put the poem in "Book." Try to trust that there's a manuscript in there somewhere.

PROMPT:
Buy a pack of cue cards or cut blank paper into squares. But really, invest in some cue cards. Cue cards are the best. You are going to be so happy that you own cue cards.

Now, open up a piece of your writing that never really went anywhere. Read through the piece, circling any words you think have potential. Be as generous with this assessment as possible. Write one of your circled words on each cue card. Now, spread the cue cards out on the floor. Start to arrange and rearrange the words until combinations of words start to sing to you; until something about the order of them feels right. Trust your instincts. You know what to do.

Once you have a basic structure in place with the cue cards, transcribe the piece into a notebook, adding all the words you need to add as you go. While I've written entire poems this way, more often than not, I come away from this process with a good line or two — a great start to a new poem.

LIFE, REVISED: COAXING AUTOFICTION OUT OF TENDER MEMORIES

CARLEIGH BAKER

I write autofiction, which can be loosely defined as a form of fiction-alized autobiography. I get to be my best self in my stories — not my most morally correct and sparkling and clever self, because who wants to read about people like that? But my characters get to flail more eloquently, cushioned by efficient, crisp language that I can't usually access while fumbling through the real world. In a 2018 article in *Vulture* magazine, journalist and critic Christian Lorentzen said that stories in this genre give readers the impression they've stumbled into the pages of the author's journal. But that impression is false and highly engineered through the revision process. Unlike most journal entries, autofiction stories are peppered with well-placed conflict. They reach the climax at the appropriate moment and provide denouement that satisfies and provokes. There are many steps to the process of nar-rativizing life, but I'd like to focus on the early stages because I find them the most challenging. Many humans, myself included, cling to our perceptions of reality, particularly when recalling emotionally charged events. Before the guidelines of narrative can be applied to a story pulled from life, a loosening of these perceptions must happen.

For me, memory is where it all begins. After identifying a juicy, conflict-heavy event from my past, I write it down exactly the way

I remember it. Some might argue that it's already autofiction at that point because memory is seldom entirely accurate. I don't wish to pick a fight with memoir writers about the veracity of their work. In fact, in her brilliant essay "Memory and Imagination," memoirist Patricia Hampl speaks to the process of recalling an important event in her life: "The work of writing personal narrative caused me to do something very different from transcription. I am forced to admit memory is not [...] a gallery of framed pictures. I must admit that I invented."

This release from the tyranny of remembered "truth" has been very helpful for my drafting process. The idea that our memories are utterly fallible and, more importantly, already turning lived experience into fiction inspires a sense of freedom that allows me to shape thoughts into story. Hampl says: "We only store in memory images of value. To write about one's life is to live it twice, and the second time is both spiritual and historical." In this way, the process of remembering can be seen as a creative process itself.

A side note here, although my chosen memories are usually fraught, which is to say, filled with conflict, I'd strongly caution the emerging writer against choosing a memory that is too fresh or deeply traumatic. Which is not to say we shouldn't write about these things. But workshopping and editing a work that comes from our most delicate emotional experiences is extremely difficult. To write about fresh trauma is to become doubly vulnerable — exposed — to outside opinions on both your writing and your life. To produce a draft on a tight deadline is asking a lot of your practice. It's not necessary to cut yourself open to tell a good story. You deserve gentleness and care.

Which is not to say writing is always comfortable. The first time I was asked about my early drafting process on a panel, I eagerly presented an image of eating cold pizza and sobbing into a wad of tissue. Then, I was embarrassed. What about long pensive walks, mugs of tea, and spirited craft conversations with other writers? Well, that stuff is great, but my process is usually pretty messy. To my surprise, my colleagues on the panel heartily agreed with me. The moderator asked audience members who considered their writing time to be less than glamorous, and many hands were raised. Vulnerability can be exhausting, but if the early drafting stage is a bit of a disaster, revision is where I eventually hit my stride.

A pivotal aspect of care during the revision process is time. After that first draft of wobbly memory dump is complete, I put it away. Sometimes for days, sometimes weeks. The distance I'll need to consider it as a story instead of a memory demands this. Not only are details of our past heavily curated by our memories, but they're filled with personal bias. Occasionally, readers sheepishly admit they didn't really like one of my me-characters, and the thing I find funny about this is the assumption that I really, truly believe I'm always likeable. Quite the opposite, really, my characters are typically selfish, self-absorbed, disaffected, or making terrible decisions. This makes for good conflict, and conflict drives storytelling. But it takes me a long time to get to the point when I can admit this. In the first few drafts, my protagonist is often completely earnest in her motivation, doing good in the world, horribly misjudged by a cruel society, wronged by loved ones, etc. This is what the pages of my journal actually look like. On mornings when writing must get done, but something's in the way of the flow, I'll unleash all my woe in the journal, and that usually releases my creativity from the claws of self-doubt. I'd be embarrassed to have anyone read my actual journal, even though what goes in there is a vital part of the process. But it's just for me.

There is a similar release that happens in the transition between memory and autofiction — the abandonment of what we remember as "the truth" and a willingness to see life as an elastic first draft. At least part of this release comes out of compassion — for myself and the other characters in my story. Imagine getting into an argument with someone. Now think about how that initial feeling of righteous anger eventually branches out into something more nuanced. Perhaps after sleeping on it, a feeling of absolute rightness may be tempered by a greater understanding of the role you played in the argument or a lack of communication that you didn't immediately perceive. You may feel empathy for the person you argued with or, if you're like me and internalize a lot of blame, you might feel greater empathy for yourself. When this expanded understanding of a situation occurs, revision can begin. We haven't reached the narrative sluice yet — making a life event conform to reader expectations of conflict, climax, and denouement. At this point, we're just working with memory in a more relaxed and liquid form. It's a place where anything can happen. In this stage — with a mindset of acceptance and empathy — elements, like character desires and motivations, can be developed.

The first story in my collection, *Bad Endings*, is about the end of my marriage. In real life, a broken relationship had dissolved, and after years of being a reclusive "housewife," I had to hustle to get a job and reintegrate with the world. The first job I got was handing out *Metro* newspapers at SkyTrain stations in the wee hours of the morning. Even as I shivered through the long, cold mornings, feeling like a failure in every sense of the word, one thought remained — this will make a great story. It had everything: good solid character "business" (handing out *Metro*s), a fantastic co-worker character (an eccentric woman who had gone through a divorce herself), and a glimmer of hope for the ending, as the end of the stifling relationship offered a possibility for my long-awaited self-actualization as a human being. I wrote down everything that came to mind: the bitter cold of a pre-dawn suburb, the rush of commuters, the smell of newspaper ink and coffee. The sensory details sang, but the characters came out flat, devoid of emotion and, more importantly, motivation. What did they want, what were they striving for? This question was particularly relevant to the protagonist — me — who needed to have a goal in order to push the story along. Her "business" goal was to hand out newspapers, but what was her understory? What did she want in the moment I'd chosen to capture in my story? Although I'd made the ethical choice not to represent my ex-husband in great detail, I needed to have similar questions answered in my mind before I could compose his character. Many tissues and pizza slices were consumed during this process.

It took a few rounds in the drawer before I realized what the story was missing. In real life, the speed at which I had to remove myself from the apocalyptic relationship required a ruthless stuffing of emotions — my survival demanded it. There was no time to consider the "he said, she said" particulars of divorce; I needed a job, a new home, and a stiff upper lip. In the process of survival, I'd distanced myself from the two primary actors in the story, my ex-husband and me, to the point of barely seeing them.

I needed to forgive these characters. I needed to forgive them for having tried to love and failed. I needed to see them as tender and fallible. It was actually easier to do for my ex-husband than for myself. But once I could see them both through a lens of compassion, I could bring them to life and study them with interest, like truly fictional characters. Gradually, the real-life details of my marriage became flexible, and the characters led me to new and unexpected places. I was writing a story on the theme of failed love with the benefit of lived experience. Again, I return to Hampl, and this statement on the old "write what you know" cliché: "I don't write about what I know: I write in order to find out what I know." Writing autofiction doesn't clarify life's dilemmas, but it does widen our perceptions. A fictional world built from imagination takes skills, but a world built from introspection takes time and heart.

PROMPT:
Write a letter to your (narrative) self.

When writing autofiction, you are the protagonist. Unsurprisingly, it can be very hard to see ourselves in the holistic, empathetic, and somewhat clinical way writers see their imagined characters. To help with this, I recommend making your protagonist a pen pal. Write them a letter (or letters), forgiving them for past mistakes. Write them with suggestions for how to deal with the conflict they're experiencing in the story. Consider your position in these letters: Are you a wiser version of yourself? A twin? Be thorough, honest, and most importantly, kind.

THE DRAFT IN THE DRAWER

BRIAN PAYTON

You wrote, you revised, you set it aside. What brings you back again?

I have a confession to make: I've poured myself into manuscripts, then allowed them to languish for years in desk drawers and computer hard drives. If this sounds familiar, it's important to remember that you are not alone. It's a dilemma faced by many writers. Some stories lie in wait of new inspiration. Others are shelved due to changing life circumstances or a lack of time to write. Writers keep these projects hidden away, out of sight but not out of mind. How do you know when to let them go or pick them up again?

Some stories that once felt "finished" reveal themselves to be works in progress or background for a new and better story. Sometimes, a writer returns to a three hundred–page manuscript, peopled with many characters, only to discover that just one of those characters rings true. That character might ultimately come to life in a new story, all her own. Other stories we return to tell us they aren't worth our continued investment. I've had to face this sad fact before. This doesn't mean that we've wasted our time or that we haven't grown by writing them. Quite the opposite. It means we've matured enough to know that the decision to park the manuscript was the right one. When your gut tells you to abandon a story, resolve to walk away with the hard-won lessons. Crystalize these lessons by writing a review. What were its strengths and weaknesses? What ultimately pulled it down? An honest assessment will help you sharpen the tools in your toolkit for the next story.

But what if you can't let it go? What if you still see it for what it *could* be?

Feedback helps in deciding whether to reengage with a story, but, ultimately, the writer must make this decision. If you're holding on to a manuscript — if you resist recycling those marked-up pages or deleting that file — it's a monument of sorts: a monument to your ambition, creativity, and determination. It could also be a monumental mess. But if there are living, breathing characters at the heart of it — if the plot, themes, or voice still draw you in and captivate you, urge you to spend time with them and in their world — pay attention. Some part of it is alive. Is it enough to save your story? Can you bring some new insight or energy to help shoulder it out of the rut you left it in?

I'm a runner, and for me, this activity has taken on metaphorical proportions in both my life and work. I get my best ideas while running and always return refreshed. Running helps define my day and reminds me that *movement* (action) also helps define character, theme, scene, plot, and narrative arc in my writing. There are short stories and novels, short runs and long runs. For me, writing a novel or book of narrative non-fiction is akin to running a marathon. When I set out, I have to pace myself and constantly stay focussed on the commitment to see it through to the end. This helps me complete a draft. Then what?

My first novel, *Hail Mary Corner*, began as a memoir. That way of telling the story failed. I set that version of the story aside and wrote it again as a novel over a period of several years. My commitment to the characters, themes, and the story itself was strong enough to see me through many, many drafts and, ultimately, to publication.

Soon after, I wrote the first draft of my second novel, *The Wind Is Not a River,* and then set it aside. Feedback helped me see that a subplot wasn't working. I tried to fix it but ultimately tore it out and rewrote the story again. I ended up setting it aside for a few more years as I was working on other stories — among them two books of narrative non-fiction — but I kept coming back to this historical novel because I couldn't let it go. I could always see its potential. The characters were real to me. Like a parent, I felt compelled to do everything within my power to ensure my characters had the best shot at life. Finally, I came back at it nine years after that first draft and revised it once again. Ten years passed between the first and final draft. That version went on to be published internationally, in five languages.

PROMPT:
What about your story? What brings you back?

It's important to identify what first drew you and continues to draw you to your story. Is it the characters, themes, plot, or setting? Untangling these motivations can help you determine next steps. Maybe you set your manuscript aside because life intervened and pulled your attention away. Be honest about your motivations for returning. Write them down. Now it's time to be honest about the story itself.

Fidelity to a flawed story should not rely solely on sheer determination. Base it on some objective assessment of the story's worth and potential. Often, that assessment can only come after having set the story aside. With an open mind and heart, read it from beginning to end. You'll want to make notes along the way, and that's fine. But now, write a review of this story. Where the review of an abandoned story is more of an autopsy, this review is as an editorial letter to yourself. An editorial letter is what professional editors provide writers before publishing their books. It is essential to be honest. What do you love about it? What kept you turning the pages? What could use some improvement? What made you cringe? Of those things that require attention, what should you cut entirely, and what can you rework? Now, make a to-do list.

If you choose this path, go big. It might give you a small sense of accomplishment to tinker with dialogue or scene-setting but avoid this temptation. Put the two or three most important items at the top of the list. Let's call them Game Changers. Go after them first. Check them off as you accomplish them. Celebrate each accomplishment. Once you've dealt with the Game Changers, accomplishing other things on your list will seem simple by comparison. After major surgery, you'll need some time away again to see if it was a success. Never forget: readers won't see all the false starts, detours, and failures along the way. They only see the final draft.

Whether you ultimately decide to recycle or recommit, facing the draft in the drawer will help you become a better writer. It might also produce a story you're proud to introduce to the world.

GIVING VOICE TO YOUR WORDS

FIONA TINWEI LAM

We writers spend most of our lives attempting to distill and transmit experience, emotion, and meaning through words. We scrutinize every phrase, rearrange syntax, shape and re-shape passages, hone myriad precise details. "To pay attention, this is our endless and proper work," as poet Mary Oliver stated. Although, as writers, we may focus on the written, we must never forget to also pay attention to the aural. The voice is a vital and potent instrument to express what we have worked so hard to craft. At a good reading, the colours, tones, and textures of the author's voice will reach every corner of the room, conveying mood, atmosphere, character, and movement. Voice and words will act in concert to create a world within a poem or story, transporting the audience on a journey that will linger long after the reading is over.

My first public reading years ago was at an open mic at an Ottawa pub. After returning to writing poetry after a long gap, I gathered enough courage to finally give it a try. I had to wait almost two hours due to the long list of regulars who'd signed up earlier. My heart was pounding, my palms sweating. I was so terrified I could barely listen to the other readers. After I read my poem, certain that no one had been paying attention, the organizer rushed up with praise, encouraging me to return. Unfortunately, I was already preparing to leave town. My shyness had caused me to miss out on participating in a thriving literary community. That same performance anxiety continued into my second reading at my first poetry retreat at St. Peter's

Abbey in Saskatchewan. Although there were less than a dozen people present, I was intimidated. The other poets there had published in books or literary magazines. I was the newbie, reading raw personal poems about my family. My throat constricted midway through a poem about my father's death. I stumbled through the rest of the reading, barely audible, my voice actively impeding the poems I'd polished over months. When finished, I fled from the room, mortified. After that retreat, I vowed I would never do a disservice to my own writing again. Becoming a better writer also meant becoming a better speaker.

Back in Vancouver, I registered for continuing studies courses to work on my voice. I started with a weekend intensive course with Langara College's Studio 58 theatre instructors and then took an improvisation course and a voice course in the evenings. As an introvert, it took me a while to warm up, but I soon became comfortable shouting, whispering, moaning, skipping, and flailing with everyone else. Listening to superb performers such as Ivan Coyote, Jillian Christmas, and Shane Koyczan taught me much about pacing and layering pathos and humour. I learned the most, though, from observing what has frustrated, disappointed, alienated, or bored listeners at events. Beautiful and powerful writing can be undermined by an ineffective reader who fails to connect with the audience.

Of course, I have made my fair share of mistakes at literary readings — misjudging travel time, trying to squeeze in too many poems, over-emoting, forgetting names, arriving late, leaving too early. But I never stop learning about what works (and doesn't work) each time I go to an event. What I have gleaned over the past twenty years can be summarized here in three main practical points: be prepared, be aware, and be gracious.

BE PREPARED

When you are preparing what to read, try to select material that will engage your audience (e.g., something compelling, curious, or humorous, a scene with action and dialogue). If you are reading several small pieces or sections, ensure there is variation in tone and content.

The background information necessary to set up your reading for the audience shouldn't be longer than the piece itself. Edit what you plan to read to suit the audience and fit the time limitations you have been given, which might mean deleting sentences, reordering scenes, or skipping passages.

Plan to read for slightly under the time allotted to allow for extemporaneous remarks. Practice your set aloud with a timer at least a few times in advance. Record yourself, so you can adjust pacing and phrasing (we often read too fast when nervous) and vary your tone to ensure that your reading will be as clear as possible. Prepare backup material in case a co-presenter reads something too similar to yours or because you discover last minute that it's not the right fit for the audience.

You can notate your text, so you know exactly what to emphasize and where to slow down, speed up, pause, and look up at your listeners. I like to circle the key images and visualize them while rehearsing so that I can later transmit aspects of those images through my voice and gestures. Remember to mark your selected passages with Post-it Notes or bookmarks, so you don't waste time searching for the pages you want. You can also have your pages stapled or in a binder to avoid embarrassment in case they fall.

Find out as much as possible about the reading in advance: who your host and co-readers will be, what the format is, whether there is a microphone and podium, and if the bookseller there will have copies of your book. It may seem obvious but getting the exact address and planning your journey are essential. You don't want to get lost, be late, or miss the event entirely. Reconfirm the details of your event in advance and obtain the organizer's telephone number in case of unexpected delays.

It's wise to arrive at least fifteen to twenty minutes early to meet the host and the other readers, do a soundcheck, find a comfortable place to sit, become accustomed to your surroundings, and get a sense of the audience. Arriving late, breathless, and frazzled doesn't presage disaster, but you will need to exert extra energy to settle yourself. (Ten long, deep belly breaths plus a few minutes of meditation can help.)

You might wish to bring your own bottle of water and a snack to the venue. Wear comfortable shoes and clothing to allow you to focus on your reading. Have a current bio handy just in case the one your host has is out-of-date. It is a good idea to have a second copy of what you want to read and to check the lighting beforehand. At one event a few years ago, the spotlight shining in my face was so blinding that I couldn't read my printout, but I could rely on a copy on my phone.

BE AWARE

Pay attention to what your body's signals are telling you so that you can do what is necessary to take care of yourself, whether it's drinking a glass of water or getting a bite to eat, taking an Aspirin, or having a few minutes of quiet time. But don't let your nerves prevent you from being aware of your audience and surroundings. Observe your fellow readers when they are at the microphone so you can see where best to position yourself for optimal sound quality.

At the venue, be conscious that you are "on" from the moment you arrive to the moment you leave. What you say and do and how you behave at the event will affect how you are perceived and received. When you are on stage, show your audience that you are aware of them by acknowledging them and giving them eye contact during your reading to foster that vital connection between writer and listener. Their reactions will tell you if your voice is too soft or too loud or if you are reading too fast.

Most importantly, be aware of time. It is essential that you stay within your allotted time. To do otherwise is a sign of insensitivity, selfishness, and neediness. You might be taking away from other readers' time. They could be stewing and fretting in the wings, their anxiety escalating. If the event is an open mic, readers might end up getting cut from the roster. There might be another scheduled event to follow, or there may be extra costs incurred for lighting and sound crew. The cliché holds true: leave your audience wanting more. Hopefully, they'll return to hear you another time or maybe even buy your book.

BE GRACIOUS

Finally, don't forget that it takes many people to put together a reading and to maintain the critical infrastructure of the writing and publishing world. Introduce yourself to your fellow readers and host and thank them at the end of the event. Take the time to acknowledge organizers, coordinators, volunteers, and the venue itself. Show appreciation for your audience. After you've read, stay to hear the other readers perform, meet fans, sign books, and debrief afterward with your host and colleagues. Forgive yourself the occasional blunder or gaffe — we all learn through our mistakes — but there is no excuse for rudeness or unkindness. You are the messenger for your own words. Consider how you want to be remembered.

I'm grateful to have attended and participated in hundreds of stimulating and engaging literary events over the years. Regardless of the prestige of the venue or the writer or the size of the gathering, the synergy between author and listener can elevate an ordinary reading into an extraordinary experience. Some of the most moving readings I've been to were held in casual settings with a small but attentive audience. Both as a reader and as a listener, I've been fortunate to feel that alchemy of intensity, authenticity, and insight. It's akin to an electrical current, as voice and words intertwine to channel something profound and universal. Those moments may be rare, but they are what we strive for: to do justice to the words we've toiled to put on the page and offer the world.

PROMPT:
1. Record yourself reading your intended piece aloud.
2. Then using different coloured highlighters or pencils (or just circles, squares, lines, arrows), note the following on the page:
   - key images
   - key verbs and verb phrases
   - dialogue, exclamations, imperatives, and questions
   - shifts in tone or mood

- where you'd like to slow down, pause, and look up
- where you'd like your voice to go up or down in pitch and volume

3. Record yourself a second time, following your notations.
4. Listen and compare. How did you improve, and how can you do even better (e.g., enunciation, pace, texture, tone)?

TOOLING AROUND THE BEFORES AND AFTERS

KEVIN SPENST

All the formal and narrative elements of poetry and prose originate in our bodies.
— Betsy Warland

How many hours a day can one devote to putting words onto a page? The intensity of concentration makes an eight-hour workday next to impossible, and besides, most of us are juggling other responsibilities and means of employment. Catherine Owen's immensely practical *The Other 23 & a Half Hours: Or Everything You Wanted to Know that Your MFA Didn't Teach You* argues that how we spend our time outside of writing can come back to inform creative work that "flourishes and sends out ecstatic and exploratory roots." While we may work towards hour, page, or word counts, we also need rejuvenation for our bodies and souls, wrists, and fingers.

In mid-April of 2020, my third book of poetry was slated for release with Anvil Press. A month earlier, on the week of March 16, literary events in Vancouver started to fall like dominos: on Wednesday, Fiona Tinwei Lam's launch of *Odes & Laments*, on Friday, a Simon Fraser University reading series at Massy Books, and on Sunday, the Dead Poets Reading Series at the Vancouver Public Library. There were plenty more, but these three events were ones in which I was involved, and as I responded to group emails, I had a sinking feeling that my launch, too, would be postponed indefinitely, lost in a long list of cancelled events.

In the first few months of COVID, I worked from home alongside my partner in our one-bedroom apartment. Like many others, we struggled to process what was happening while also trying to get work done through the transition to a mostly online existence. (And yes, in this, and so many other ways, we've been extremely fortunate.) I reanimated my body jogging the trails of Stanley Park and found myself spending more and more time around a large moss garden hidden off of the main trails where varieties of liverworts, hornworts, and mosses flowed over stone spirals and undulations of the forest floor. One afternoon, I cleared leaves and twigs from a patch of forest nearby, and a couple of days later, I dragged together moss-covered branches to create a perimeter around the clearing. I had no idea what I was doing, but it felt good to move my legs and arms after hours sitting in front of my computer writing or lying on the couch under the glare of my phone. Then, on one morning run, I stopped and started filling in the green perimeter with sticks, rocks, and swatches of moss fallen from the mammoth maples. My fingers and clothes grew dirtier as I lost myself in hour after hour making something that I only realized was a stage many days later. This giant web of green was where I would launch my book, *Hearts Amok: A Memoir in Verse*.

That week, the provincial government announced that people could meet in small numbers. I invited a poet friend to open for me along with a couple of other friends to make up an audience of five. The more I thought about the reduced risks of being outdoors, the more I toyed with doing multiple readings outside. Finally, after some prep work and support from my partner, who agreed to do the filming for Facebook and Instagram, we launched my book on May 20 at ten pop-up venues outside friends' homes from East Vancouver to the West End. The final reading took place deep inside Stanley Park, and the day ended in a glow of ecstatic exhaustion.

"I learn by going where I have to go," writes Theodore Roethke, and I think poetry helps us cultivate hunches. I wake to write most mornings, but I try to balance routine with an awareness of what my body has to say. In *Rules for the Dance: A Handbook for Writing and Reading Metrical Verse*, Mary Oliver writes: "A cardinal attribute of breath (or breathing) is, of course, its repetition. The galloping footbeats of the heart, that spell fear. Or the slow and relaxed stretch of breath of the sleeping child. In either case, by their repetition, they make a pattern. Truly this pattern is as good as a language." I write and write and stop to listen to my breath, and there are times its rushed shallowness tells me that my mind and body are out of sync. If, as Betsy Warland suggests in *Breathing the Page: Reading the Act of Writing*, "[c]ompelling writing emits from embodiment: provokes embodiment in the reader," then we need to remember how breath bears both body and mind.

The modern world has splintered us into smaller and smaller anxieties in its insistence on pieces and parts, atoms, and abstractions. If I sit down to write from a small place in my head that only thinks in pieces, rushing past the fullness of the emotional and physical, my words will fail to bring the fullness of the world to the page. Words will feel asphyxiated and flat. When I find the time to meditate, jog, and listen deeply to others, that is, listening from what Thomas Merton calls "the ear of your heart," my writing expands in its connections. I love writing and reading when it's done in the fullness of embodiment: when I'm physically and emotionally engaged.

From the success of my outdoor readings for *Hearts Amok*, I did thirty more, but when rain forced me to cancel an afternoon of pop-ups, I took the time to doodle through a copy of one of my books. It was as if my pen was illustrating my unconscious. After posting photos of this doodled edition, a dozen people expressed interest in having their own copy. I spent the next couple of days letting my hand wander and drift in drawings through a dozen copies of my book. Less Virginia Woolf's "when the pen gets on the scent" and more cartoonist Lynda Barry's "drawing as a side effect of something else: a certain state of mind that comes about when we gaze with open attention."

What do we do before and after we write? We dance, sing, hike, and camp (here I think of Bren Simmers's latest book, *Pivot Point*, a poetic rendering of a canoe trip through the Bowron Lake Canoe Circuit). We take photos (here I'm thinking of multi-genre author Hiromi Goto's Twitter account, where she posts nature photos with the hashtag #ALittleBeautyEveryDay). We make visual art (author Carrie Jenkins's drawings and paintings are also on Twitter under #carriedrawsstuff). We learn other languages (Ian Williams's poem "Tu me manques" explores the syntax differences between English and French). And we collaborate (poet Brandon Wint does audio recordings of his work with producer Jeepz). We build up our confidence to play with the tools of our craft, and through everything, we try to understand as much as we can in as many ways as are available to us. Most importantly, we breathe, and in the seconds that sync everything together, we marvel at how (in the words of Betsy Warland) "[a] luminous moment can contain years of lived experience."

And we breathe again.

PROMPT:

Outillage Autour des Avant et Après

In her essay "Thirty Recommendations for Good Writing Habits," Lydia Davis suggests that authors learn at least one foreign language. She quotes *How to Survive the Coming Collapse of Civilization: And Other Helpful Hints* by Sparrow, who writes, "It doesn't matter which language you study. What's important is confronting words like *szökik* (Hungarian for 'jump')."

If you can devote the time to work on another language, there are many excellent resources online. What's particularly exciting is that you can dive into the realia of another language. From time to time, I listen to the news in French, and I watch movies and Netflix series in order to keep my French going. There are also language instructors such as Hugo, whose podcast series at innerfrench.com is highly entertaining. The more French I learn, the more I can read and be inspired by other voices, and the more words I have to include in my own writing.

Even dabbling in other languages can spur the start of a character or setting for a story or an occasion for a poem: a Hungarian whispering *"szökik"* into their phone, a German crying *"Kummerspeck"* ("grief bacon") towards the sky, or a Turk talking about *"Gumusservi"* (a word that means "the reflection of moonlight on water"). Unraveling the why will take you somewhere new.

If you don't have the time to learn another language, or even about another language, one exercise I learned in a workshop taught by poet Katia Grubisic is to take a poem in a language you don't know and do your best to "translate" it; that is, play with the impressions that the words leave you with. This will nudge you in new directions.

Engaging with a new language places us in the humbling position of not knowing. Speaking new words that slowly become familiar allows us to understand our mouths and bodies in different ways. Some basic fluency in another language opens up new conversations with others and helps us learn a fraction about some of the other billions of people on this planet. "To imagine a language means to imagine a form of life," wrote the philosopher Ludwig Wittgenstein, and every word plays some part of that life, which can lead to new shapes in your writing.

PUBLISHING AS ALCHEMY

LEIGH NASH

I've been the publisher of Invisible Publishing since the end of 2015; it's a role I've been both consciously and unconsciously working toward for the better part of a decade and is, absolutely, my dream job. Invisible is intentionally small, in that we publish about ten books each year, and our mission is to treat every title like a lead title, whether it's a novel or collection of poetry or essays. As a small press publisher, I wear many hats: I edit manuscripts, set budgets, pack boxes, and sell books. I also feel Invisible's success and failures acutely; it's my job to learn from them in order to more effectively shepherd their books out into the world.

Given this, I also feel a sense of responsibility to mentor the authors I'm lucky enough to work with. I love the collaborative energy that emerges in the author-editor relationship, and my hope is that authors come away from the process with a better understanding of their writing, of editing, and of publishing as a whole. There's a lot of work that goes into making each book during the journey from Microsoft Word document to paperback, but there's also a combination of skill, creativity, timing, and luck. It's more than a little like alchemy.

Nigredo
The manuscripts that convince me to offer a contract for publication with Invisible are often very different than the books we end up putting out into the world. The writing, of course, is the most important part of the process — it allows the writer to craft their true vision for

the book, to hone their voice, to write the story they want, or need, to get down on the page. But submitting a book to a publisher is really just the beginning. I treat publishing as alchemy, a mix of craft and magic, and the manuscripts that stand out are the ones that are wholly original and seem to come alive off the page.

When I'm reading a manuscript for the first time, I first look for a way in — I need to understand the work at its core to begin to see the possibilities in it. I try to determine whether an author and I can work together on publishing the best book possible, to create the author's own personal philosopher's stone: a work of writing that they believe in, that will stand the test of time.

Albedo

A start can be tentative: *I Am a Truck* by Michelle Winters was waiting in the slush pile when I took over Invisible. I loved the voice from the first page, but I didn't love the book's structure. It was divided into three sections centered on each character, and it was too long. Still, I could see the shape of the story, that it might work better to have all the narrative threads woven together, to play with the structure. I shared all of my feedback over coffee with Michelle before I offered her a book contract; I wanted to see if she'd be interested in doing the work it'd take to get the manuscript to where I thought it could go.

I think it's crucial, especially when working on significant revisions, for a writer and editor to be on the same page. Editing is a trust exercise, with the author falling backwards into the editor's arms — sometimes you stick the landing, and sometimes you both come crashing down, but there are beautiful moments in either scenario.

Michelle blew me away with her initial round of revisions and continued to do so through every pass, even as I continued to suggest she kill her darlings. There's nothing more magical than an author rejecting an editorial suggestion only to do something bigger and better and bolder, something beyond what you've imagined. That's the power of collaboration, of conspiration, of editing — bringing light and clarity to story. In this case, the book found its readership:

I Am a Truck was a finalist for the 2017 Scotiabank Giller Prize, has been translated into German, and kicked off Michelle's literary career.

Citrinitas

Conversely, a start can be a leap of faith. Andrew Kaufman's *Small Claims* came to Invisible with the title *Petty Justice*, and it was originally proposed to be an essay collection based on his *Hazlitt* column of the same name, in which he'd written about his visits to observe trials at small claims court. The essays morphed during the editorial process (Invisible author Stephanie Domet worked with Kaufman on the substantive edits) into one cohesive non-fiction book — with the court visits linked together by a loose narrative — and then into the novel we eventually published. It's a departure from Kaufman's other magical-realism novels, an outlier in his catalogue; at its core, *Small Claims* is a realistic novel about searching for humanity and love and redemption.

Sometimes the path through acquisitions, editing, and production is straightforward, and sometimes it meanders, turns corners, or ends up parked on a bench for a bit — every book's path through the process is unique. It took two years for Kaufman's proposed book to work through the various iterations and find its way onto store shelves, which is both a long and a short time in the book world. Never once did I think about not publishing it, even though the project went through a total transformation — we'd committed to the book and the writer, and, in every conversation we had throughout the process, Kaufman became more confident about the story. In the end, it's a book I'm really proud to have published: it's an example of an author taking a risk to step outside his comfort zone.

Rubedo

Writing is such a solitary act, and publishing is such a communal one; they initially seem at odds but are really complementary. Midway through the editing process, when a book is torn apart and everything is laid bare — that's where I often pause, take a deep breath, and hope I've given my best advice, that I haven't steered the author wrong or somehow turned the book into a disaster.

Sometimes a book has to completely fall apart in order for the author to bring it back into harmony. Projects shapeshift, grow unrecognizable and unfocused from one draft to the next, until they suddenly snap into clear view, beautiful and whole.

The process from first draft to final reader unfolds differently for every author, and the job of an editor — and publisher — is to provide a steady hand throughout the process of transmuting ideas into books. It's like spinning straw into gold or turning lead into silver: it's mysterious, unknowable, hard work — but it's also completely magical.

PROMPT:

A manuscript can change shape/focus/form during the editing and publishing process, and for a writer, such big shifts might initially feel destabilizing. To better envision the possibilities for your project, here's a trio of editing/revising experiments:

1. Swap genres and transform a poem into an essay or vice versa.
2. Shift perspective and rewrite from a different point of view by turning a main character into a sidekick or a bystander into the protagonist.
3. Reshuffle the timeline so that the end becomes the beginning or your novel gains a new organizational structure.

OUT IN THE DEEP END

BRIAN KAUFMAN

Okay, you've worked hard and you've finished that manuscript and now you're wondering what to do with it. Even though book publishing is an industry dominated by transnational interests, I believe it is easier for writers to get published today than at any other time in the history of book publishing. But you need a plan. So much of getting published — and by "published" I mean published by the *right* publisher for your book — depends on matching your manuscript with the appropriate publisher.

Given how few unknown authors are signed up by the big houses, you are more likely going to be shopping your manuscript to one of the many small- or medium-sized independent presses in Canada or the U.S., and there are dozens of them to choose from.

If you truly believe that you have a book that is going to change the world, a book that has huge, mainstream appeal, then get yourself a good agent, hold out for a contract with one of the Bigs (or one of their dozens of imprints) and try to make that vision a reality. If you don't and you settle for a deal with a smaller indie publisher and the book fails to light the world on fire, you'll be plagued by the *"What if..."* for the rest of your life. But if the waiting and hoping turns into years, you may want to consider other options and avenues to publication.

One such avenue is that of the independent publisher. If you have a manuscript that is ready to be hugged between two loving covers and make its way into the world, then you have some choices to make. As I mentioned earlier, there are dozens of independent publishers across the country and, for the most part, they all have their own special area(s) of focus — their niches — and are chiefly interested in receiving manuscripts that are a fit for their mandate and publishing program. Study their websites and review closely the areas in which they publish, eg: poetry, drama, young adult, historical fiction, work with LGBTQ2S+ themes, etc. And take particular note of what they do *not* publish. Eighty percent of the manuscripts we "decline" at Anvil are not necessarily bad ideas for books or poorly written works, they are simply not a fit for our list. Choose and target your publisher carefully; read their submission guidelines closely; then read them *again* and do exactly as they request.

Once you have selected your target publisher (or a handful of publishers), compose a concise cover letter that will intrigue and capture the attention of the editor or publisher opening the mail. Don't bore them; cut to the chase — tell them who you are and what it is that you have to offer in a direct one-page cover letter that will make that person want to read the sample you're sending. Remember, many indie publishers are small-staff operations and they receive *hundreds* of manuscripts and proposals every year. Do everything you can to elevate your submission above the dozens and dozens of others that you are competing with. All publishers are captivated by a strong voice, a great opening line, a great first paragraph, a great first page. Don't let cliches and sloppy, derivative language kill your chances of being noticed (and getting published).

The Publisher/Author relationship, once established, will be a partnership, two teams working together to make your book and its foray into the world the most rewarding experience as possible. Approach publishers with this in mind. Your publisher wants your book to do well; every publisher wants to see every book they publish sell thousands of copies, they want to applaud your every success.

This bit of advice is only intended as a primer for your journey into conventional print publishing. Writers today have so many alternate avenues to explore and from which to launch their writing: online magazines, personal blogs and websites, self-publishing services such as Lulu, Reedsy, or BookBaby, or maybe you want to explore the world of Crypto Writing and NFTs. Whichever route you take, you have to build an audience, develop a readership for your work, or you have to hire someone to help you do that. The best option I can think of is to sign up with a hard-working team at a small publishing house who make the promotion of your work an integral part of the publisher-author relationship. It is not enough to mount your writing at a website or a blog and expect curious thousands to show up and read and/or purchase your book. As you know, online competition for eyeballs and clicks is immense. Why *your* roadside attraction on the internet highway over the hundreds of thousands of others? You and us and everyone else in the writing and publishing world are up against huge conglomerates that are constantly jockeying for a larger slice of the pie. We are all competing for attention, and vying for the same entertainment dollars. This is the modern world of writing and publishing and who knows what new platform may arrive tomorrow that will change all the rules of the game.

Whatever direction you choose, put on your trunks and wade on into the crowded pool; it's not that scary, even out here in the deep end.

PROMPT:
Try writing a concise and engaging synopsis of your current writing project — poetry collection, novel, memoir, collection of short stories or essays, whatever it might be — in 250 words or less. And once you've done that, try condensing it down to an "elevator pitch" — a one paragraph description of the work that will entice an editor or publisher to want to see the entire manuscript.

NOTES ON PUBLISHING LITERARY BOOKS

ANDREW STEEVES

¶ I have tried to publish and market literary books like a subsistence farmer raises and sells the food they produce, while the mainstream of trade publishing has come to have more in common with commercial feedlots and the global supply chains they enable. My approach arose from thinking about the extraordinary thing that books are and how they function in our communities.

¶ When I've interviewed candidates for jobs at the press, I've often asked some version of the question: *what is literary publishing for?* I ask this question because it speaks to motivation, and understanding our motivation seems like an essential first step in understanding our actions.

I don't know why other people choose to work in literary writing and publishing, but my motivation for publishing literary works, and doing it with the uncommon care that I do, is aligned with my life-long interest in journalism. I think that publishing literature is an equally valuable tool, if more indirect and lyrical, than news report-ing if your desire is to produce work that informs, equips, and supports the community. It is a tool that might ultimately penetrate more deeply and whose impact might be felt over a longer period, longer than a news cycle. It is a tool that fosters the discussion of more nuanced and complex ideas. I publish literary books because I think that they help the community to understand what is happening to it, and through it, and provide a means for articulating what it is like to be alive, here, in this place, in this time.

I also value the way that literature fosters robust thinking. Surely the reader who can wield metaphoric language, parse a complex phrase, or re-expand the compacted imagery of a work of fiction into a vivid and complex universe in their mind is also likely to be someone who can wield robust arguments against injustice, parse environmental reviews or development regulations, or imagine a way forward for a community faced with difficult decisions. The skills that literature nurtures and exercises are the very skills necessary for our everyday lives as citizens. Without the robust kind of thinking and communication that a healthy literary culture enables, the coherence of the human world suffers, and with it, our ability to understand our relationship with the world at large.

¶ Books are also interesting in and of themselves, as tools and as objects. They are a rather recent innovation, a retrofit, a complex and imperfect embodiment of more elemental, more organic methods of communication such as storytelling. Over millennia, as language took physical form and moved from the tablet to the scroll to the codex, the production and circulation of books evolved into its own intriguing cultural-technical phenomena distinct from the "story" itself, accumulating rich traditions for managing the myriad practical riddles of arresting and communicating a text, riddles that are perpetually in need of solving, page after page, book after book. As tools that transmit cultural information across time and space, books inhabit the fault line between the static and the dynamic word; as words are thought, written, typeset, printed, and read, humans are participating in the animation of the culture. The words awaiting us in the book are charged, and when read, are discharged; this process can happen over and over. Something about the book's form, when executed with skill and with care, seems uniquely suited to its cultural purpose. In thinking about why I publish literary books, I realize that I'm not just motivated by the things that books can *do*, but also by the kind of thing that they *are* in the world as objects.

¶ I find a great deal of pleasure in publishing books. There is the Border collie's pleasure of bunching up so many unruly details and herding every last one of them through the gate. There's the technician's pleasure of mastering arcane skills and wielding them to tilt the normal temporal limits of things. There is the pleasure of giving physical form to abstract things. There is the risk-taking and speculating, and the way they sometimes pay off. And there's the satisfaction of selecting good texts and engaging with their authors, of bringing forward works you feel might have a lasting impact on the community. Most of these are pleasures that are also pleasurable *per se* in the moment of their enactment and not particularly dependant upon external validation. This seems to me to be an important element of both publishing and writing — pleasure.

¶ What good books can do for the community; the kind of lithe thing that a well-wrought book is; the kind of pleasure found in doing useful work well — these are all things I'd want writers to understand about the way literary publishing can potentially function in the culture.

Come to think of it, these are things I wish more *publishers* understood about literary publishing. If they did, they might take a deeper interest in their trade and produce better books. Too few contemporary literary publishers have any real sense of the history of the field predating their own entrance into it. Too many neglect the physical properties of their books rather than investing care in them: jamming vital cultural texts into indifferent bodies ill-suited to their purpose, treating books as a mere delivery mechanism for commodified information and entertainment on par with the blandest and stalest of cones ever to hold ice cream.

What I wish more writers understood about book publishing is that too many publishers are ignorant of, or indifferent to, their cultural responsibility to make good and useful things, to publish books in a way that enables the community to understand and articulate its daily life. As writers and readers, if we want a publishing industry that produces books in a way that is as robust and culturally enriching as the texts they embody, we must actively encourage it by interrogating the motivations of our publishers and assessing their level or commitment to our community and its needs and its values. To do otherwise is to abandon literary publishing — and the book — to a much diminished cultural role.

¶ Many bad manuscripts get published while many good ones get passed up, so one ought to avoid using publication as a measure of a work's value; when value gets conflated with commerce and culture, it's a crazy morass. The value to an author — and potentially to their family and community — of writing something down ought not to be undermined by a rejection letter from a publisher. Not everything of value is of public interest; nor can everything of value be packaged and sold.

¶ When I select literary projects for publication, I focus on picking interesting, original works that I feel will enrich the community, projects that I believe our press is properly equipped to produce and sell. It's really that simple. A publisher pursuing bestsellers or prizewinners makes much more complex, but no more certain, calculations.

¶ When reading the covering letter to a manuscript submission, I don't much care about who the author took a workshop with or who mentored them. Just show me the goods. While it creates good employment for a few, the Creative Writing Industrial Complex is not really the whetstone for writing that it claims to be. As the recipient of hundreds of the manuscripts emerging from these programs annually, I can tell you that the Creative Writing Industrial Complex appears to dull many more blades than it sharpens. Originality is what's wanted, alongside clarity, to make a manuscript jump out in the submissions pile, and yet these common writers' supports seem more successful at fostering uniformity.

¶ Somewhere in the vast riches of Boswell's *Life of Johnson* is a footnote that attributes the following sentiment to Dr. Johnson: *Never trust anyone who's written more than they've read.* My perennial advice to aspiring writers is simply to read widely and to engage with the people and the world around you; writing finds its way along behind those things, when it finds its way at all.

¶ In fiction, good dialogue is important but hard to write; I think in part because we are readily fooled into believing that we have written it well — it *seems* so easy. I have read few novels in which dialogue makes up the greater part of the work that engaged me profoundly enough to draw me back to re-read them. On the other hand, I can think of many narrative passages in fiction — like the wolf hunt in Tolstoy's *War and Peace* or Wendell Berry's description of his protagonist's overnight trek through the flooded Kentucky countryside in *Jayber Crow* — that are vividly lodged in my imagination and draw me back to those books. With every passing year, the number of fiction submissions I receive that read like a television script grows, and the number of submissions that confidently handle rich narrative diminishes.

¶ I worry that each rejection letter I write will be the end of the road for the project, that the author will despair and give up on their own work. Because I receive so many submissions each year, I end up declining the majority. But many of the projects could well be published — by me or by someone else — and many more show promise but require extensive revision or a fresh start. One of the reasons I handwrite all my rejection letters is that I want to humanize the news, to put my decision into properly modest proportion. My disinclination is a pronouncement of nothing more than my interest or ability to participate as the work's publisher: *I appreciate the offer. I could not use this. What you are trying to do has value. Keep going. Don't ever lose heart.*

¶ A society in which many people are observing what's going on around them and trying to express what they discover — directly or indirectly — as art is infinitely preferable to one where everyone has abandoned such pursuits for passivity or malice. In art, and in the pursuit of art, lies much potential for nurturing empathy and understanding. In literature, we work out who we are to each other.

THE STORIES WE TELL

BRIAN LAM

My career in publishing started off in a not entirely uncommon way: as a dream of becoming a writer. I studied creative writing at the University of Victoria, focusing on short fiction, under the tutelage of such fine writers as Jack Hodgins and Leon Rooke. Looking back, I realize that none of my stories featured characters who looked like me: a queer Asian man. This being the early- to mid-1980s, there was no tangible collective consciousness about cultural representation; despite the adage of writing about what you know, perhaps my own lack of self-confidence made me believe that no one would be interested in stories about people who looked like me. So, my stories were populated by non-racialized (i.e., read as white), straight, cisgender folks with their (white) straight, cisgender problems.

It was after I moved to Vancouver and began working at Arsenal Pulp Press — first as an office manager, then moving tenuously into publicity and then editing — that I started to feel more confident and aware of the kind of stories and poems I wanted to read and help publish. Arsenal had a gonzo reputation of sorts in those days, in the best sense of the word. It was a casual, renegade outfit of anti-establishment literati. Their loose energy, not bound by the old traditions of CanLit, made me realize I had found my place in the world, not by writing my own stories, but rather by helping to bring the work of others into being. In those early years, I met writers and editors — people much braver than me — who were not only comfortable in their own skin but actively dedicated to sharing their stories about what it means to be "othered," whether racialized or queer (or both), and to be empowered by that sharing. Randy Fred, the founder of Theytus Books and a residential school survivor who ran our Tillacum Library imprint of books on Indigenous issues, taught me about the power of storytelling to heal. Jim Wong-Chu, who created the Asian Canadian Writers Workshop as a way to encourage young writers, revealed to me how uncomfortable stories and poems about the racist past can bring communities together. And queer writers and editors Dennis Denisoff, James C. Johnstone, and Aren X. Tulchinsky (formerly known as Karen X. Tulchinsky), and queer booksellers Jim Deva and Janine Fuller, showed me the power of literature to galvanize the LGBTQ+ community, reined in by institutional homophobia and devastated by AIDS, into political action and social change.

Twenty-five years later, in the shadow of the disgraceful Trump presidency and its tragic consequences, I am convinced more than ever that the stories of the "othered" need to be written and heard. These stories are not just for the communities that are being written about; they are, and should be, for all of us. Everyone should read the novels about the gay Cree sex worker (Joshua Whitehead's *Jonny Appleseed*), the queer Nigerian émigré (Francesca Ekwuyasi's *Butter Honey Pig Bread*), and the emotionally messy thirty-something trans woman (Casey Plett's *Little Fish*), among others, because these books show us the importance of empathy and respect. For writers, this means having the confidence to reveal your own truth in your work, no matter how personal or uncomfortable. In 2000, Ivan Coyote published their first story collection *Close to Spider Man* with us. Their disarmingly straightforward and quiet prose about growing up genderqueer in the Yukon has, over the years, moved thousands of readers: from queer youth to straight grandmothers. Amber Dawn has written novels and poetry on her experience as a former sex worker. Her award-winning memoir *How Poetry Saved My Life* is a groundbreaking book for its emotional intimacy, revealing how literature can be a virtual lifeline. When Lindsay Wong first sent her memoir *The Woo-Woo: How I Survived Ice*

Hockey, Drug Raids, Demons, and My Crazy Chinese Family to publishers across Canada, she was told that no one would want to read a book about a Chinese Canadian family with mental illness. But the book has gone on to win numerous awards, it was a Canada Reads finalist, and it has been praised for offering a unique racialized perspective on mental illness. In their books, Ivan, Amber Dawn, and Lindsay had the courage to own their own truths, and they stood steadfastly by them despite the prospect of adverse criticism or harm.

Looking back, I wish I had their kind of self-confidence when I was biding my time as a writer-in-training on my way to becoming a publisher. For those of you who are writers or who wish to be, bravery is a required trait, but it's more than that — it's the willingness to dig down deep to find truths that you haven't necessarily discovered about yourself before and the commitment to share those truths with others. For BIPOC and LGBTQ+ writers, especially those who have never felt empowered to acknowledge those truths, this can be an unsettling prospect. But find yourself a shovel, take a deep breath, and start digging. Because we need to hear your stories.

CONTRIBUTORS

Caroline Adderson is the author of five novels, two collections of short stories, and many books for young readers. Her work has received numerous award nominations, including the IMPAC Dublin Literary Award, two Commonwealth Writers' Prizes, the Governor General's Literary Award, the Rogers Writers' Trust Fiction Prize, and the Scotiabank Giller Prize longlist. Winner of three BC Book Prizes and three CBC Literary Prizes, Caroline is also the recipient of the Marian Engel Award for mid-career achievement. She teaches in the creative writing program at Simon Fraser University Continuing Studies and is program director for the Writing Studio at the Banff Centre for Arts and Creativity.

Joanne Arnott is a writer, editor, arts activist, originally from Manitoba, at home on the west coast. She received the Gerald Lampert Memorial Award (League of Canadian Poets, 1992) and the Mayor's Arts Award for Literary Arts (City of Vancouver, 2017). She has published six poetry books, a collection of short non-fiction, and a children's illustrated. Recent publications include her third poetry chapbook, *Pensive & beyond* (Nomados Literary Publishers, 2019), and the co-edited volume, *Honouring the Strength of Indian Women: Plays, Stories, Poetry* by Vera Manuel (University of Manitoba Press, 2019). She is a poetry mentor in the Writer's Studio at Simon Fraser University and poetry editor for *EVENT* magazine. *joannearnott3.blogspot.com*

Peter Babiak lives and writes in East Vancouver. A collection of his essays, *Garage Criticism: Cultural Missives in an Age of Distraction*, was published by Anvil Press in 2016 and nominated for the Eric Hoffer Book Award the following year. Two of his essays were selected for the *Best Canadian Essays* anthologies in 2017 and 2018. A regular writer of commentary-based essays for *subTerrain* magazine, Peter teaches linguistics and literature at Langara College.

Carleigh Baker is a nêhiyaw âpihtawikosisân/Icelandic writer and teacher who lives on the unceded territories of the xʷməθkʷəy̓əm, Sḵwx̱wú7mesh, and səl̓ilwətaʔɬ peoples. Her short stories and essays have appeared in numerous journals and have been anthologised in Canada and the United States. Her debut story collection, *Bad Endings*, won the City of Vancouver Book Award and was also a finalist for the Rogers Writers' Trust Fiction Prize and the Indigenous Voices Award for Most Significant Work of Prose in English by an Emerging Indigenous Writer. She was a 2019/2020 Shadbolt fellow in the humanities program at Simon Fraser University, where she now teaches creative writing.

Joanne Betzler graduated from the Writer's Studio at Simon Fraser University in 2013 and has several writing projects underway, including a second novel, historical fiction based on her great-grandmother, a poetry collection, and a handful of personal essays. They all remain on hold until she finishes managing the complexities of her memoir. She juggles her time between words, gardening, and her cohabitation family bubble, which includes her husband Grant, two of her grandchildren, their parents, and two dogs. Connecting with other writers as a manuscript consultant at her local library (through SFU's writing consults), writing workshops, and timed writing sprints with friends keep her focused.

George Bowering, Canada's first Poet Laureate, was born in the Okanagan Valley. A distinguished novelist, poet, editor, professor, historian, and tireless supporter of fellow writers, Bowering has authored more than eighty books, including works of poetry, fiction, autobiography, biography and youth fiction. His writing has also been translated into French, Spanish, Italian, German, Chinese, and Romanian. He has taught literature at the University of Calgary, Sir George Williams University, and Simon Fraser University, and he continues to act as a Canadian literary ambassador at international conferences and readings. Bowering has twice won the Governor General's Award, Canada's top literary prize.

Claudia Casper is the author of *The Mercy Journals*, winner of The Philip K. Dick Award, the bestseller *The Reconstruction*, and *The Continuation of Love by Other Means*, finalist for the Ethel Wilson Fiction Prize. Her creative non-fiction has appeared in *Dropped Threads*, edited by Carol Shields and Marjorie Anderson, and *Geist* magazine, among others. Her most recent short fiction, "Walt's Head," was commissioned by *subTerrain* magazine. Claudia is a speculative fiction mentor in the Writer's Studio at Simon Fraser University. She lives in Vancouver, BC.

Janie Chang writes historical fiction that draws from a family history with thirty-six generations of recorded genealogy. Her novels are inspired by family stories about life in a small Chinese town and tales of ancestors who encountered dragons, ghosts, and immortals. Her debut novel, *Three Souls*, was a finalist for the 2014 Ethel Wilson Fiction Prize; *Dragon Springs Road*, her second book, was a *Globe and Mail* national bestseller. Both were nominated for the International DUBLIN Literary Award. Her third book, *The Library of Legends*, was also a *Globe and Mail* national bestseller.

Andrew Chesham directs the Writer's Studio at Simon Fraser University, and is the long-time publisher of the annual *emerge* anthology. His work has appeared in magazines in both Canada and Australia and is a regular presenter at literary conferences and festivals. Andrew is the editor of *From the Earth to the Table* and *Stories for a Long Summer* (Catchfire Press). He is working on his first novel.

Wayde Compton has written five books and edited two literary anthologies. His collection of short stories, *The Outer Harbour*, won the City of Vancouver Book Award in 2015, and he won a National Magazine Award for Fiction in 2011. His work has been a finalist for two other City of Vancouver Book Awards as well as the Dorothy Livesay Poetry Prize. From 2012 to 2018, he directed the creative writing program in Simon Fraser University Continuing Studies. Compton is currently the chair of creative writing at Douglas College in New Westminster, BC.

Eileen Cook is a multi-published, award-winning author with her novels appearing in nine languages. Her books have been optioned for film and TV. She spent most of her teen years wishing she were someone else or somewhere else, which is great training for a writer. She's an instructor/mentor with The Creative Academy and the Writer's Studio at Simon Fraser University, where she loves helping other writers find their unique story to tell. Eileen lives in Vancouver with two very naughty dogs.

Claudia Cornwall has written seven books. *Letter from Vienna: A Daughter Uncovers Her Family's Jewish Past* won the Hubert Evans Non-Fiction Prize. *At the World's Edge: Curt Lang's Vancouver, 1937-1998* was a finalist for the 2012 City of Vancouver Book Award. *Booklist* picked *Catching Cancer: The Quest for Its Viral & Bacterial Causes* as one of the best books of 2013. It was shortlisted for the Canadian Science Writers' Association Book Awards. Claudia's most recent book, *British Columbia in Flames: Stories from a Blazing Summer*, was published in 2020 by Harbour Publishing. Claudia is a non-fiction mentor in the Writer's Studio at Simon Fraser University and lives in North Vancouver, BC.

Kayla Czaga is the author of *For Your Safety Please Hold On* (Nightwood Editions, 2014) and *Dunk Tank* (House of Anansi Press, 2019). Her writing has appeared in numerous magazines and anthologies — including *The Walrus, Plenitude Magazine, Maisonneuve, Canadian Notes & Queries,* and *The Best of the Best Canadian Poetry in English* — and has been awarded *Arc Poetry Magazine*'s Poem of the Year award, *The Fiddlehead*'s Ralph Gustafson Poetry Prize, and *The Malahat Review*'s Far Horizons Award for Poetry. She holds an MFA in creative writing from the University of British Columbia and lives in Victoria, BC.

Leanne Dunic (she/her) is a biracial, bisexual woman who has spent her life navigating liminal spaces, inspiring her to produce trans-media projects such as *To Love the Coming End* (Book★hug Press/Chin Music Press, 2017) and *The Gift* (Book★hug, 2019). She is the fiction editor at *Tahoma Literary Review* and the leader of the band The Deep Cove. Her latest book is a lyric memoir with music entitled *One and Half of You* (Talonbooks, 2021). *leannedunic.com*

Laura Farina is the author of two full-length books of poetry, *Some Talk of Being Human* and *This Woman Alphabetical*, as well as the chapbooks, *Diagnostic Tool* and *Choose Your Own Poem*. She's also the author of the picture book, *This is the Path the Wolf Took*. Laura is the recipient of the Archibald Lampman Award, and has appeared on the longlists for both the ReLit Award and the CBC Poetry Prize. She coordinates the Writer's Studio at Simon Fraser University, and creates writing for social engagement projects as part of The Imprint Collective.

Raoul Fernandes lives and writes on the traditional territories of the Musqueam, Squamish, and Tsleil-Waututh Nations (Vancouver, BC). His first collection of poems, *Transmitter and Receiver* (Nightwood Editions, 2015), won the Dorothy Livesay Poetry Prize and the Debut-Litzer Award for Poetry in 2016 and was a finalist for the Gerald Lampert Memorial Award and the Canadian Authors Association Literary Award for Poetry. He has been published in numerous literary journals and anthologies, including *The Best of the Best Canadian Poetry in English*.

Joan B. Flood grew up in Limerick, Ireland, and lived briefly in France and England before settling in Victoria, BC. Her poetry, short fiction, and non-fiction have been published in Canadian, American, and Australian anthologies. *New Girl*, a young adult novel, won the Orpheus Fiction Contest and was published in the U.S. Her story "87" won honourable mention in The Binnacle's Ninth Annual International Ultra-Short Competition in 2012 (U.S.). *Left Unsaid*, her adult novel, was published by Signature Editions. *joanbflood.com*

Janet Fretter is a writer and editor. A member of Editors Canada, she offers freelance editorial services for emerging and established writers of fiction and narrative non-fiction. She is a graduate of the Writer's Studio (TWS) and the Editing Certificate programs at Simon Fraser University. She presents topical writing workshops, both privately and through TWS Community Workshops. From 2014 to 2017, she served as managing editor of *emerge*, the annual anthology produced by the students of TWS. She continues a strong connection to this creative community.

Stella Harvey's short stories have appeared in *The Literary Leanings Anthology, The New Orphic Review, EMERGE Web Magazine,* and *The Dalhousie Review.* Her non-fiction has appeared in *Pique Newsmagazine, The Globe and Mail,* and the CBC. Signature Editions published her first novel, *Nicolai's Daughters,* in 2012, and Psichogios Publications of Athens published the Greek translation in 2014. Signature Editions published *The Brink of Freedom* in 2015. *Finding Callidora* is Stella's third novel. Stella founded the Whistler Writing Society, which produces the Whistler Writers Festival and other literary programming under her direction. She is the memoir and personal narrative mentor in the Writer's Studio at Simon Fraser University.

Paul Headrick is the author of a novel, *That Tune Clutches My Heart* (finalist for the Ethel Wilson Fiction Prize), and a short story collection, *The Doctrine of Affections* (finalist for the Alberta Book Award for Trade Fiction). He has also published a textbook, *A Method for Writing Essays about Literature.* Paul taught creative writing for many years at Langara College and gave workshops at writers' festivals from Denman Island to San Miguel de Allende, Mexico. He is a mentor for a graduate narrative workshop with the Writer's Studio at Simon Fraser University.

K. Ho is a writer and photographer living on the unceded territories of the xʷməθkʷəy̓əm, səl̓ilwətaʔɬ, and Sḵwx̱wú7mesh nations (Vancouver, BC). Their work explores bodies, desire, and absence. They are a 2018 VONA/Voices fellow, a graduate of the Writer's Studio at Simon Fraser University, and a first-year MFA candidate.

Aislinn Hunter is an award-winning novelist, poet, and educator. She is the author of eight books, including *The World Before Us* (winner of the Ethel Wilson Fiction Prize) and her most recent novel, *The Certainties* (Knopf Canada, 2020). In 2018, she served as a Canadian war artist. She teaches creative writing at Kwantlen Polytechnic University and at Simon Fraser University in the Writer's Studio.

Reg Johanson has been teaching writing and literature for almost thirty years, the last twenty at Capilano University in North Vancouver, on Squamish and Tsleil-Waututh territory. He was an editor for CUE Books, and his writing has recently appeared in *The Elephants, The Capilano Review,* and *Best Canadian Stories 2018.*

Joseph Kakwinokanasum is a member of the James Smith Cree Nation. He is a graduate of the Writer's Studio and the Writer's Studio Graduate Workshop at Simon Fraser University. He was shortlisted for the 2020 CBC Nonfiction Prize. His work has been published in *The Humber Literary Review* (2020 summer issue) and in *emerge 18: The Writer's Studio Anthology* (2018). For his manuscript, "Woodland Creetures," he was awarded the 2014 Canada Council for the Arts creation grant for aboriginal peoples, writers, and storytellers. *starblanketstoryteller.ca*

Brian Kaufman has been active in the publishing community as a writer, editor, and publisher for over thirty years. Mr. Kaufman is the founder of Anvil Press and *subTerrain* magazine and has been the recipient of the Jim Douglas Publisher of the Year Award and the City of Vancouver's Mayor's Arts Award for his "significant contribution to Vancouver's arts and cultural community."

Jónína Kirton is a Red River Métis/Icelandic poet and a graduate of the Writer's Studio at Simon Fraser University, where she later served as the BIPOC Auntie supporting and mentoring BIPOC students. A late-blooming poet, she was sixty-one when she received the 2016 City of Vancouver's Mayor's Arts Award for Literary Arts in the Emerging Artist category. Her first collection of poetry, *page as bone - ink as blood*, was released with Talonbooks in 2015. Her second collection, *An Honest Woman*, was released in 2017, again with Talonbooks, and was a finalist for the Dorothy Livesay Poetry Prize.

Brian Lam is the president and publisher of Arsenal Pulp Press, a book publishing company based in Vancouver. He is a former president of the Association of Book Publishers of British Columbia, a former board member of the Association for the Export of Canadian Books (now Livres Canada Books), and currently serves on the board of the Association of Canadian Publishers. He won the Community Builder Award from the Asian Canadian Writers' Workshop in 2014, the Ivy Award from the Toronto International Festival of Authors in 2018, and the Publishing Professional Award from Lambda Literary in the U.S. in 2020.

Fiona Tinwei Lam has authored three poetry collections (*Intimate Distances*, *Enter the Chrysanthemum*, and *Odes & Laments*) and a children's book (*The Rainbow Rocket*). She also edited *The Bright Well: Contemporary Canadian Poems about Facing Cancer*. She has collaborated on award-winning poetry videos that have screened internationally. Shortlisted for the City of Vancouver Book Award and thrice selected for BC's Poetry in Transit, her work appears in over forty anthologies, including *Best Canadian Poetry* (2010, 2017 anniversary edition, and 2020). She was recently appointed Vancouver's sixth Poet Laureate. *fionalam.net*

Jen Sookfong Lee was born and raised in Vancouver's East Side, and she now lives with her son in North Burnaby. Her books include *The Conjoined*, nominated for the International DUBLIN Literary Award and a finalist for the Ethel Wilson Fiction Prize; *The Better Mother*, a finalist for the City of Vancouver Book

Award; *The End of East*; *Gentlemen of the Shade: My Own Private Idaho*; *The Shadow List*; and *Finding Home: The Journey of Immigrants and Refugees*. Jen acquires and edits fiction for ECW Press and co-hosts the podcast *Can't Lit*.

JJ Lee's memoir pieces and personal essays have appeared in *Maclean's*, *ELLE Canada*, and *MONTECRISTO Magazine*. His memoir, *The Measure of A Man: The Story of a Father, a Son, and a Suit*, was a finalist for the Hilary Weston Writers' Trust, Charles Taylor, and Governor General's prizes for non-fiction. Every Christmas, he writes and records a holiday ghost story for broadcast and/or podcast. He lives in New Westminster, BC.

Katherine McManus, Ph.D., is an instructional designer, teacher, and writer. She has been involved in adult education as an administrator, programmer, advocate, and researcher for over twenty years. Currently in retirement, she continues to teach and write. She also volunteers in various professional organizations.

Christina Myers is a writer, editor, and former journalist. She is the creator and editor of the non-fiction anthology *BIG: Stories about Life in Plus-Sized Bodies* (2020) and author of the novel *The List of Last Chances* (2021). She juggles creative work and parenthood from her home in Surrey, BC. *cmyers.ca*

Leigh Nash is the publisher of Invisible Publishing, a small, scrappy, and seriously good independent Canadian publishing house. Her past experience includes jack-of-all-trades-ing at Coach House Books, overseeing Marmora's dogsledding festival, and building Re:word Communications, an editorial firm, from the ground up. She has an MFA in creative writing from the University of Guelph and is the author of *Goodbye, Ukulele*.

Brian Payton is the bestselling author of *The Wind Is Not a River*, which was published internationally and chosen as an Amazon Book of the Month, an Amazon Canada Editors' Pick for Best Fiction of the Year, and a "Best Book of the Year" by the *Seattle Times* and *BookPage*. Previous works include the novel *Hail Mary Corner* and two acclaimed works of narrative non-fiction: *Shadow of the Bear: Travels in Vanishing Wilderness*, which was a Barnes & Noble Book Club Pick and a National Outdoor Book Awards Book of the Year, and *The Ice Passage: A True Story of Ambition, Disaster, and Endurance in the Arctic Wilderness*, which was a finalist for the Hubert Evans Non-Fiction Prize.

Maria Reva writes fiction and opera libretti. She is the author of the linked story collection *Good Citizens Need Not Fear*, shortlisted for the Atwood Gibson Writers'

Trust Fiction Prize. Her stories have appeared in *The Atlantic, McSweeney's, Granta, The Journey Prize Stories, The Best American Short Stories,* and elsewhere. Maria was born in Ukraine and grew up in New Westminster, BC. She received her MFA from the Michener Center for Writers at the University of Texas.

Renée Sarojini Saklikar's ground-breaking poetry book about the bombing of Air India Flight 182, *children of air india: un/authorized exhibits and interjections,* won the Canadian Authors Association Award for Poetry and was shortlisted for the Dorothy Livesay Poetry Prize. Her book *Listening to the Bees,* co-authored with Mark L. Winston, received the 2019 Gold Medal in the Environment/Ecology category of the Independent Publisher Book Awards. Renée was the first poet laureate for the City of Surrey (2015-2018) and served as the 2017 University of British Columbia Okanagan Campus Writer-in-Residence. She curates Lunch Poems at Simon Fraser University and the Poetry Phone (1-833-POEMS-4-U). Renée's work has been adapted for opera, visual art, and dance. Her sci-fi poetry epic *THOT J BAP* is forthcoming in 2021.

Madeline Sonik is a multi-genre writer, anthologist, and academic. She holds an MA in Journalism, an MFA in Creative Writing, and a PhD in Education. Her books include a novel: *Arms*; short fiction: *Drying the Bones*; a children's novel: *Belinda and the Dustbunnys*; and two poetry collections: *Stone Sightings* and *The Book of Changes*. Her volume of personal essays, *Afflictions & Departures,* was a finalist for the Charles Taylor Prize and won the 2012 City of Victoria Butler Book Prize. Her latest book, *Fontainebleau,* is a linked story collection.

Kevin Spenst is the author of the poetry collections *Ignite, Jabbering with Bing Bong,* and *Hearts Amok: A Memoir in Verse* (all with Anvil Press) and over a dozen chapbooks, including *Pray Goodbye* (The Alfred Gustav Press), *Ward Notes* (the serif of nottingham), *Surrey Sonnets* (JackPine Press), and, most recently, *Upend* (Frog Hollow Press: Dis/Ability Series). He occasionally co-hosts *Wax Poetic: Poetry from Canada* with RC Weslowski, Lucia Misch, and Zofia Rose on Co-op Radio. He lives in Vancouver, BC on unceded Coast Salish territory.

Andrew Steeves founded Gaspereau Press in 1997 (with Gary Dunfield). He spends his time reading, writing, editing, designing, typesetting, printing, binding, marketing, selling and talking about books. His most recent project is the limited-edition letterpress book *Literarum Ex Arboribus: An Exuberant Showing of the Wood Type* at Gaspereau Press, a three-year undertaking that resulted in the creation of over 150 wood type specimens.

Candie Tanaka is a multiracial trans writer and artist who was born in Vancouver, BC, and grew up in the small town of Tsawwassen. They are a graduate of the Writer's Studio at Simon Fraser University and also Emily Carr University of Art + Design in Vancouver, BC. In 2017, they were the recipient of a fully funded literary residency at Banff Centre for Arts and Creativity that helped them further push the boundaries of their writing practice. They've recently completed their first fiction manuscript and are currently busy working on their second.

Rob Taylor is the author of *Strangers* (Biblioasis, 2021) and three other books of poetry. He is also the editor of *What the Poets Are Doing: Canadian Poets in Conversation* (Nightwood Editions, 2018) and guest editor of *Best Canadian Poetry 2019* (Biblioasis, 2019). He teaches in the creative writing program at Simon Fraser University Continuing Studies and lives in Port Moody, BC with his wife and children.

Betsy Warland has authored thirteen books of creative non-fiction, essays, and poetry. *Lost Lagoon/lost in thought* was published in 2020. A seconded edition of *Bloodroot: Tracing the Untelling of Motherloss* (with a new long essay) comes out in 2021. A mainstay for writers and teachers, a second edition of *Breathing the Page: Reading the Act of Writing* (with newly added material) comes out in 2022. Former director and mentor in the Writer's Studio at Simon Fraser University and Vancouver Manuscript Intensive, Warland received the City of Vancouver Mayor's Arts Award for Literary Arts in 2016. Warland works as a freelance manuscript mentor and editor.

John Whatley has been, variously, a lecturer at Simon Fraser University (SFU) in English literature, an academic program director specializing in remote learning (retired), and is currently the managing editor of SFU Publications. He was at one time a poet (and might yet be one), has presented papers at numerous conferences, and published critical articles and one book: *Voicing the Essay: Reading and Writing for Depth* (2013). From 1989-2021, John taught courses on crime and literature, the literary essay, Canadian fiction, the English and German Romantic periods, the Gothic and Romantic in world literature, poetry, and the scope of the Gothic novel. He has taught in the SFU Department of English, the SFU Department of World Languages and Literature, and the Anglistik Fachbereich, Justus Liebig Universität in Germany. He is currently focused on the relation between the rise of the essay as a literary form and the rise of the novel.

ACKNOWLEDGMENTS

We would like to extend our genuine appreciation to everyone who helped in the production of this book. Christina Myers' insight and tips, early in the process, helped guide us in bringing together a wide selection of voices. Tamara Jong provided production support and her usual can-do attitude. Janet Fretter provided sound, thoughtful editing advice. Brian Kaufman believed in the project and collaborated with us, helping shape the list of contributors and then trusted us to develop the book. Derek von Essen provided beautiful cover art and book design. If one thing shines through in these essays it's that writers create best when they are supported by community. We'd like to thank ours: Kiran Dhanoa, Betsy Warland, Wayde Compton, Shanthi Besso, Katherine McManus, Megan Frazer, Lifelong Learning at SFU, and the Writer's Studio.

THE WRITER'S STUDIO

Many of the writers featured in this anthology are part of the community that surrounds The Writer's Studio (TWS), a mentorship program at Simon Fraser University. Founded in 2001, the year-long cohort program matches students with a mentor and a workshopping group. Each year, these writers are featured in the Studio's anthology, *emerge*. TWS also offers short-term courses and workshops open to anyone, including: multi-week courses and one-day, low-barrier workshops. Free monthly activities include: the TWS Reading Series, Lunch Poems, Mini-Manuscript Consults, Twitter Chats and Sprints, and the Zoom Writing Space. All writers and readers are invited to join these community events.

TWS has multiple scholarships to help writers enter our year-long cohort, including emerging writers, writing moms and Black, Indigenous and writers of colour. Proceeds from the sale of each book will go to support these scholarships.

For more information about the Writer's Studio's community activities or to learn more about the program, visit: *SFU.ca/write* or Twitter: *@twssfu*